An Invitation
to Classical Sociology

An Invitation to Classical Sociology

Meditations on Some Great Social Thinkers

Franco Ferrarotti

LEXINGTON BOOKS

Lanham • Boulder • New York • Oxford

LEXINGTON BOOKS

Published in the United States of America
by Lexington Books
A Member of the Rowman & Littlefield Publishing Group
4501 Forbes Boulevard, Suite 200, Lanham, Maryland 20706
www.rowmanlittlefield.com

PO Box 317
Oxford
OX2 9RU, UK

British Library Cataloguing in Publication Information Available

Library of Congress Cataloging-in-Publication Data

Ferrarotti, Franco.
　An invitation to classical sociology : meditations on some great
social thinkers / Franco Ferrarotti.
　　p. cm.
　Includes index.
　ISBN 0-7391-0508-6 (hardcover : alk paper)
　1. Sociology—History. 2. Sociology—Philosophy.　I. Title.

HM461.F47 2002
　301—dc21　　　　　　　　　　　　　　　　　　2002012392

Printed in the United States of America

⊗™ The paper used in this publication meets the minimum requirements of
American National Standard for Information Sciences—Permanence of Paper
for Printed Library Materials, ANSI/NISO Z39.48–1992.

Contents

Preface

✝

An Invitation to Classical Sociology: Meditations on Some Great Social Thinkers

I have been writing these essays over the past ten to fifteen years, essays ranging from Adam Ferguson, the great theorist of the seminal concept of "civil society," to Thorstein Veblen, the radical critic of American society and well-known author of *The Theory of the Leisure Class*. This collection of essays lends itself to at least a double use. On the one hand, it can serve as a general introduction to the history of social thought, where each author is considered within his specific historical context and where he takes up the basic questions posed by his own society. On the other, this book can also be described as an interpretation of various social thinkers that is highly personal and linked with a distinctly European approach to social philosophy and sociology. In this case, sociology is not conceived as an excessively narrow or specialized science but rather as a general scientific examination of social phenomena. It is in this sense that these essays reflect and rest on a multidisciplinary approach; for that reason, they can be read as a valuable instrument for introductory classes of sociology as well as for a more critical and advanced study of this field of learning.

University of Rome
"La Sapienza"
Italy
Franco Ferrarotti

Introduction

A n author becomes a classic, to put it bluntly, if and when he or she has "class." This means that such an author has given ample evidence to be able to tackle the major issues of the times in complete autonomy, without being on the payroll of anybody or of any institution, with a personal empathy that does not exclude the necessary critical distance. To the classical sociologists their discipline could never be reduced to or conceived as a mere technique of itself. It is true that the number of scholars who think of themselves as sociologists is impressive; chairs and courses in sociology are active in most universities all over the world. But a great victory can at times amount to a great danger. Huge achievements in terms of organization do not ensure substantive gains. It seems that sociology has forgotten the basic lessons of its own classics. During the past fifty years sociology has missed its chance at least twice: first, on the occasion of the end of the Cold War, with the crumbling of the Berlin Wall in 1989 and the collapse of the Soviet Union in 1992; second, with the attack on the Twin Towers of the World Trade Center in New York on 11 September 2001.

It is the fact that sociology as a general field of learning, by the end of the twentieth century, appears to be theoretically timid, as if paralyzed by the magnitude of newly developing historical events. For the past fifty years—the Cold War period when East and West would confront each other squarely and uncompromisingly—global, politically motivated and oriented ideologies have had the upper hand. The global ideological outlook has undoubtedly been able to use a modicum of sociological expertise in terms of making more functional, or for purely "lubricating" purposes, the ever more complex organizational setup of the "social system." However, as a general rule, all-pervading ideologies have firmly retained the right, and the privilege, to indicate the meaning of history and the main direction of its development. Actually, the ideological mind has for years presumed to be able to map in a detailed way and to understand in all its implications the historical experience even before it took place. By the sheer force of "dialectical" anticipation, it was bold enough to conceive and to present itself as an infallible means to determine the various steps of the future historical sequence and to explain their relative function. In this connection, the role of sociology has been by definition ancillary.

No wonder the collapse of the ideologies has left sociology orphan, as it were, deprived of any major theoretical thrust. The same can be said after 11 September 2001. At the very moment in which the role of sociology would have been essential to help U.S. public opinion understand that we were moving into a world of interdependence, social science scholars were too cautious and did not feel like criticizing the typically American ambivalence between domination and the compulsion to retire into "splendid isolation." It was not understood that the historical destiny of the only remaining superpower did not consist in pointing to an apocalyptic nightmare of "clash of civilizations" but rather to a sober, pragmatic problem-solving approach for which sociology was apt to play an essential role. This was the second chance that was lamentably missed by most sociologists.

An intrinsic weakness, moreover, should be mentioned here, at least in passing. Actually, one should not overlook the fact that confusion between theory as such—that is, a specific "glance" (*theorein* in Greek means "looking") over a specific social issue—and a model-building activity still prevails. The outcome is regrettable and inevitable: sociology is downgraded to sociography, that is, description and collection of raw data without any theoretical orientation. Hence the lesson of the classics again emerges as essential.

Looking at the phase of sociological development following the end of World War II, one is likely to be struck by the breadth and substantive richness of works such as *The Lonely Crowd* and *Faces in the Crowd* by David Riesman and associates, *The Political System* by David Easton, as well as, ten years later in 1960, *The End of Ideology* by Daniel Bell. This is not to say that in the more recent period we cannot count on major pieces of work. It would perhaps be sufficient to quote the names of Jürgen Habermas and his *Theory of Communicative Action*, of Alain Touraine, with his *Production de la société*, and especially of Jeffrey Alexander and his four-volume *Theoretical Logic in Sociology*. These efforts do certainly have special merits, but also leave one uneasy. Alexander especially, who on the one hand is well aware of the importance of a "return to the classics," does not seem able or willing to escape the easy commonplace on the basis of which it would be plausible that the whole development of sociological thought since Auguste Comte has no other function than to pave the way to Parsonian structural-functionalism.[1]

I am not prepared to share the severe strictures by Richard Münch, branding recent American sociology as mere "junk food." Naturally, Münch's words should not be taken literally. But his statements are sweeping. In his article Münch simply dismisses all home-grown American sociology as junk food: "American sociology in pure geographic terms does not consist entirely of McDonaldcized products; it also offers French, German, and Italian 'cuisine' to the specialists. . . . European sociology . . . now has indigenous McDonalds, simply because of the domination by American sociology."[2] As we can see, the reaction on the part of some European sociologists to what could be presented as "American sociological imperialism," is quite harsh.

At least for some aspects, it seems hardly tenable. However, without taking into serious consideration the nutritional value of junk food, it is a fact that even among sociologists who consider themselves "incurable theorists," as Parsons did, the sad confusion between "models" and "theories" is still dominant. Whenever theory is conceived and reduced to a model or type, theory is inevitably "de-historicized." The historical dimension is simply eliminated from the research process. Theory then is "uprooted," as it were, as far as the specific historical context is concerned and social research, "freed" from any kind of historical consciousness, presumes to be able to find out the "evolutionary universals," timeless and spaceless, of any possible society. The difference between theory and model-building activity is blurred to the point of not understanding that, if it is true that a model or type is more manageable than any substantive theory, the fact remains that, although endowed with a certain degree of internal congruity, a model is essentially a purely intellectual and arbitrary construction.[3]

From this point of view, it is rather easy to understand why sociology was not able to take advantage, notably at the end of the 1980s, of the breakdown of global ideologies. Between the global ideology in crisis and the malaise of everyday life, it seems that there is a vacuum which should be filled by the sociological culture, or by the "third culture," to use the formula invented by Wolf Lepenies to show a way out of the contradiction between the scientific and the humanistic cultures.[4]

Science pervades our whole way of life. But it can hardly be forgotten that science and its practical application in the form of technology are, at best, a perfection without purpose. In other words, the rationality that goes with science and technology is a formal, not substantive rationality.

The value of science and technology to humankind cannot be disputed, but it would be sadly erroneous, as Max Horkheimer has most recently argued, to forget that it is an instrumental, not a final or substantive value. Technology can control the correctness of its internal operations. It cannot evaluate them in view of a desired eternal social goal.

Strange as it may seem, perhaps the only major thinker of the past century that actually managed to conceive and elaborate the social role of science is the official founder of sociology, Auguste Comte. Far from being a lonely and mysterious enterprise, as the popular imagination still has it, science in Comte's view fulfills a basic social role and is a determining force in modern society. Again, such a role is not merely instrumental. It has to do with the legitimating basis of modern industrial society insofar as this legitimation cannot be referred to tradition or to metaphysical or theological values but is necessarily based on scientific knowledge. What defines modernity is precisely the new concept of science—no longer a solitary initiative nor an esoteric, mysterious knowledge for the "happy few" but the social foundation of any society that is daring enough to embark upon a process of renewal, cutting off its centuries-old values and beliefs.

For Comte, science is not only knowledge to be conceived as the product of "idle curiosity," to use the famous phrase of Thorstein Veblen; it is knowledge in terms of social process, planning, and initiative. How is this possible? The main lines of Comte's reasoning are simple enough. His teacher, Saint-Simon, had stated that "mankind is not suited to live in ruins; it needs certainty and stability." After the French Revolution, mankind—*l'humanité*—had to rebuild its habitat; society needed a total reconstruction. New values had to be discovered and formulated to functions as the basic presuppositions for the various social groups. Where could these values come from? Tradition was moribund. Old-fashioned theology and speculative philosophy had little, if anything, to offer. Individual wills, on the other hand, were too unpredictable and drastically differentiated to provide a common basis for the new community; social consensus had to be founded on a totally new basis. Here Comte's contribution emerges as a stroke of genius. Individual wills are anarchistic in nature and not to be trusted. But science, on the contrary, has an intersubjectively binding value. Science does not depend on individual principles of preference. Science is a public procedure. It convinces with the pure force of reason. It can act as the new basis for social consensus.

With science as the basis for social cohesion and as the binding force of the new community, the historical process which had begun with the early phases of "industrial revolution" seems to have reached its logical outcome. It had been aptly observed that historians used to call it the Industrial Revolution; some social scientists label it modernization; the economic anthropologist Karl Polanyi termed it the "Great Transformation"; Marxists called it the transition from feudalism to capitalism. But by whatever name it has been known, scholars of all sorts have been fascinated with the emergence in the last part of the eighteenth century of the great industrial or capitalistic market economies of the Western world. Now with the collapse of communism in the former Soviet Union and Western Europe this fascination has been given new relevance. In its struggle to invent capitalism and market societies in the present, does Eastern Europe have anything to learn from the way it originally happened in the West? The answer is not a comforting one. Great historical experiences cannot be easily exported at will; however, a profound, critical assessment of what happened in the West can perhaps be useful today to the new emerging countries and developing economies all over the world.

What has to be understood—and what seems to have escaped most commentators and analysts—is the *new social function of science, and of technology as applied scientific knowledge*. We still talk and think having resort to eighteenth-century philosophical, economic, and political categories— from capitalism to socialism—and do not seem to realize that the new social realities can no longer be accommodated within these categories. The ideological conceptual framework of the eighteenth century is obsolete. It must be realized that science, scientific knowledge, and technology as applied science are the new faces of social and political power. It is not enough to talk in terms of information. The concept of information-society is at most a stepping-stone in the right direction, but it leaves the question of a full understanding of the new society open. Naturally, information plays an important role. But then an important question needs to be asked: what kind of information? Information per se is elusive and points to a blurred reality. It must be conceived and elaborated as *scientific information*—that is, verified, controllable information.

The role of information in present-day developing societies is crucial. Information has become the essential precondition of human development. During the eighteenth and nineteenth centuries exploitation of man by man was direct and more or less precisely quantifiable. It had to do with the derogation of muscular energy, working hours, wages level, factory discipline. The scenario today is vastly different. The description of the first book of Marx's *Capital* is no longer tenable. The variables are isolation, segregation, solitude, neglect, and exclusion. To be exploited in the modern world means to be on the fringes, to be cut off. Our everyday experience and common sense might seem to contradict this statement. Mass media continue to spread all over the world. Decisions at all levels of organized association are more numerous, more clamorous, more widely known. But access to a center where these decisions are taken is more difficult. The center is remote. Its arbitrary nature is consecrated by mystery, it is even hard to determine where exactly this center is located and who forms part. The message of power risks becoming Kafka's "message of the emperor." Let us set aside the philosophical and sociological theories by which the various power elites defend themselves. Then a curious and, in many ways, unexpected fact must be pointed out. Power today exploits and oppresses not by the use of direct action, which can be objectively and logically assessed on the basis of the aims in view and the results effectively obtained, but simply by ignoring, by failing to intervene, by refusing to take action, by taking refuge behind complex and perfectionist procedures through which legal formalism and political paralysis come to each other's aid. The most serious sins of power today are sins of omission. The genuine reactionary today is not the person who has a gallows erected or applauds the censor but the one who prevents action, who preaches resignation at all costs and urges others to put their trust in a spontaneous, automatic evolution and practices a "benign neglect."

In this connection, social information has at least three basic functions: a) *it prevents popular initiative from dying away* as the result of bureaucratic complications and static self-enclosed institutions; b) *it guarantees,* up to a point, *the effectiveness of the pressure from below* as a major democratic instrument capable of ensuring people's participation in the process of social transformation; c) it tends to maintain *a degree of contact between political decisions and the aspiration of the citizens,* protecting them against both authoritarian rashness and paternalistic tendencies.

These three functions cannot be fulfilled by a generic social information but by a type of information based on scientific analysis. It is here that we can fully understand the new role of science as a socially meaningful enterprise as well as the great contribution of Auguste Comte and his motto *Savior pour prévoir; prévoir pour agir*. Science, and techniques as applied science, that is, technology as the general description of the variously interconnected scientific domains and techniques, are essential for the perception and interpretation of present-day society. This society cannot be merely described as an information society. One needs to be more precise. It is a society based on scientific information: an information that is *intersubjectively binding*. A society today can be capitalist or socialist or cooperativist or based on a mixed economy from an ideological and institutional point of view. However, the underlying fundamental criteria for its definition go beyond these external features. Such criteria point essentially to the way and to the degree in which science and technology, conceived as applied science, tend to shape its structure and its basic developmental orientation. In this perspective the importance of science as such, of science in its broadest meaning to include natural and social, or moral, science, becomes clear and the famous polemics, which we mentioned above, about the "two cultures" loses much of its value.

The statement by C. P. Snow is well known. My feeling is that it has been grossly overrated. To understand the full impact of modern science one should perhaps take into account the concept and practice of science in classical antiquity. After the successful defense of his hometown, Syracuse, Archimedes burned his notebooks with the practical lessons from his experiments. The classical scientist did not have much appreciation for practical, useful application. Slaves were available in great numbers. One did not have to have resort to mechanical labor-saving devices. Moreover, among scholars the fear of menial contamination was widespread and had an arresting effect. It has been properly remarked that Greek science did not arrive at a great technological development because *it did not want to reach one*. In classical antiquity and during the Middle Ages, the scientist keeps quiet, and by keeping quiet science makes the State, the political and religious powers, afraid. It wins respect, if not money. Once in a while, the scientist is persecuted, tortured, or killed, but in general he is able to preserve his freedom. It is a fact that the men of power can live, fight, and actually be powerful only as far as the means offered by scientific culture are available. Even the tribal chief depends on the witch doctor.

As soon as science becomes something different and more than pure speculation and the scientist cannot be seen any longer as a secluded, solitary *privat Gelehrter*, or *doctus privatus*, and he seems ready to offer his knowledge for social use, especially in the growing field of industrial production, the situation changes. Already Leonardo is willing to work for the princes and for the king of France with his war machines. The scientist is no longer independent. He has traded his autonomy for a position close to power and for the material means to conduct his research. He is no longer a loner; he works more and more in groups, is part of an organization. The process of "deification," as it were, of science, already traceable to the early Middle Ages, does not correspond to any special illumination of individual scholars shut up in their cells. It rather corresponds to a compelling question of the society, which is being transformed. The correlated crisis in the fall of traditional criteria of judgment, the new horizons opened by the contacts and paths of communication with other unknown continents, the lessening of the basic legitimacy of the powers which had made themselves exclusive in social terms, had at first reduced and then undermined the ancient legitimating presuppositions of important political and social decisions. The authority of the "eternal yesterday" had been called into question. Once traditions as a source of legitimacy had fallen, to whom could one turn? Where could one identify a new instrument of self-listening and self-direction for societies which were so adventurous or imprudent as to enter onto the paths of modernization on a vast scale? Where to find a new basis of social consensus?

Science was the almost obvious answer. It was said that the cultivation of science was an act of homage to God, insofar as it permitted the study of nature, God's own creation. Newton considered God the Supreme Architect, the "pantocrator" and guarantor of the cosmic order. However, modern science seems to possess a unique hubris, a thrust whereby it does not limit itself to reflect nature. It proposes to imitate nature but at the same time it invades it, it exploits nature and reinvents it to the point of violating it. Thus the humility of the scientist as regards nature is an apparent one: it is a tactical move to disarm the adversary and take him by surprise. Bacon had said, *Natura nonnisi parendo vincitur*. But Bacon's "obedience to nature" was only the humility that precedes and prepares the triumph over and against it.

The "sanctification" of science found an unexpected reinforcement in the Puritan ethic, which was based on utilitarianism and on the idea that all knowledge should be evaluated, contrary to the wisdom of the classics, on the basis of its utility. In fact, it was thought that everything which helps make the life of man happier and less hard is good in the eyes of God. Naturally—and on this point the utilitarian and Victorian moralities were logical to the point of cruelty—this is to be understood as applying only to all those who deserve it or who pay for their welfare and their "good standing in the community" through methodical daily labor, diligence in undertaking their professional duties, and total dedication to their task. Thus the whole social life, both individually and collectively, is permeated by scientific spirit and rational calculation. Instrumental reason, as Max Horkheimer would call it, at present has the upper hand in the already developed societies and in newly developing countries.

It could be said that Auguste Comte is finally enjoying some sort of posthumous revenge. Science and scientists were supposed to serve the exiting powers. And in fact, they do serve. But in so doing, they condition rather heavily power and power-holders. The very source of power and the ways in which power is being exercised are more and more deeply affected by science and technology. Even traditional property rights—such as the private property of invested capital— are undermined by science to the point of fast becoming obsolete as power prerogatives. In large enterprises there is a clear divorce at present between the power stemming from legal property rights and the power from effective everyday control of operations. Moreover, capitalism can no longer be defined simply by taking into account its rational bookkeeping methods, as Max Weber maintained. After the collapse of so-called real socialism in Eastern Europe and Russia, capitalism can be defined even less in Werner Sombart's terms as a merely "predatory enterprise."

When compared with its classics, present-day sociology lags behind. It is successful, but it is not free. It is on the market, ready and willing to be sold to the highest bidder. But in this way, instead of developing a coherent research strategy aiming at an understanding of society as a global entity, sociology gets dispersed, fragmented, and eventually lost in a variety of petty researches according to the short-range needs of dominant market forces. Moreover, the classics were not following and had no ear for intellectual fad. They certainly were not afraid of solitude. To most of them could be applied the famous verse of Alfred de Vigny that somebody thought quite fitting for Thorstein Veblen: *J'ai vécu puissant et solitaire.*

This is not navel-watching. This is no invitation to solipsism or to uncritical "reflexive sociology," as Alvin W. Gouldner would have it. For the classics, the object of sociology is not sociology, but social problems as independently defined and analyzed by the individual researcher. In this sense, sociology is what it has historically been, and the sociologist is not only a supposedly value-free commentator or a detached interpreter but a witness who is directly involved in the social process and knows that every researcher is at the same time a "researched" person. The standpoint is inevitable for the simple reason that one cannot see simultaneously everything all the time. Sociological knowledge is a historically contextual knowledge. Value-premises are inevitable and have to be made explicit at the beginning of any social research.

In this connection, a final lesson from the classics deals with the study of humanity as historically conditioned beings who are neither totally free nor completely determined. The fundamental category here is the concept of "possibility": human being as a developing, dynamic subject within given objective circumstances. Here the shortcoming of purely intellectualistic dilemmas reveals their sophistic nature. The idea we mentioned earlier about the two cultures—humanistic and scientific—seems to be alien to our classics and, at any rate, does not lead anywhere. Actually, it ends up denying the very concept of culture in its proper meaning, that is, culture as a human problematic awareness that includes both the natural and the mental spheres of experience. However, that contrast is reflected rather unexpectedly on another level. Usually one hears people talking and even writing about the supposed tension between basic, or pure, science and applied science. No clear-cut separation between pure science and applied science is logically possible or experimentally advisable. In terms of actual research work, the two kinds of science are closely interrelated or, more precisely, interwoven. Fundamental theoretical tools and conceptual framework have often been found and raised during practical, experimental work, whereas no true scientific experiment nor fieldwork can be conducted without an explicit preliminary theoretical guidance.

The main reason for such simplistic dichotomy between pure and applied science is not to be found in any intrinsic logic of scientific research. It comes from the outside. It has to do with the usual haste coupled with a typical unawareness of the financial sponsors of scientific ventures. I am not referring only to the fragmented requests for hard scientific data and forecast coming from the extreme variety of private interests in industry and business. I have in mind the vast and powerful bureaucracies of political parties, pressure groups, labor unions, and so on. Research is called upon to supply data that would give policymakers a good chance to cloak with scientific jargon decisions that usually have already been taken before the scientific data are available. This amounts usually to an exercise in petty rationalization. Science is then used as a polemical weapon vis-à-vis rivals and competitors.

It is a different story when science works for the government or for an international agency, sponsored by various governments. A strange paradox seems then to take place. Science is undoubtedly a tool for government and at the same time government and its power are somehow coerced into its service. Between science and power a curious master-servant relationship develops. One has to go back to Hegel: the servant serves his master but by serving his master the servant little by little empties him, makes him devoid of any original initiative like an absentee owner, reduces him to a pure façade and finally replaces him. Government grants money to science to achieve certain goals, to conduct a given set of research without knowing technical details and procedures and therefore without effective control. Thus science de facto dictates in the end to government what to do, and how. No control is possible without actual knowledge. In the end, policymakers, despite all their rhetoric, are powerless when squarely faced by scientists.

The new emerging society, in this respect, cannot be labeled either as a postindustrial society or as a postmodern society or purely and simply as a "knowledgeable society."[5] Even less, can present-day technically advanced societies be defined in terms of "communicative action," as in Habermas, or as societies "produced" by debates, or *débats* as in Touraine.[6] According to Robert E. Lane, there are five characteristics that define the knowledgeable society: 1) the basic beliefs about man, nature, and society itself are constantly examined and called into question; 2) criteria for judgment are supposedly based on a tested therefore public and not merely private truth; 3) a considerable amount of resources is devoted to research; 4) collected data are continuously updated, interpreted, and organized; 5) this accumulated knowledge is officially used to clarify values and goals of the global society.

It seems that all these characteristics point to a common feature—knowledgeable societies have a great interest in knowledge. Whoever would judge this statement to be a vulgar truism, would certainly deserve to be dealt with lightly. Perhaps too many analysts are prone to state the obvious with an air of discovery. There is no doubt about the increased social significance of science in modern society. To think that the problem of interpretation of this society is solved by calling it "science" or "knowledge" or "knowledgeable society" begs the question. The object to be explained becomes the key to the explanation. The great problem of technically advanced present-day societies remains unsolved and looms large for all the marvelous scientific exploits at the beginning of the third millennium.

Knowledge, all types of knowledge, including strict scientific knowledge, are not per se self-revealing. Like technology, knowledge cannot be regarded as a *deus ex machina* to be called upon to solve the society's problems that very often it has itself contributed decisively to create. Like technology, scientific knowledge, which has created it, is not only, as Heidegger would speculate, the eternal return of the identical. It is essentially perfection without purpose. In other words, it has a mere instrumental value. Then the basic question to ask is: knowledge from whom? For what?

We are thrown back to the underlying problem of power and its substantive legitimacy and its value-orientation. Science can clarify the issues, calculate the relative costs of the various alternative courses of action, show the best ways to implementation. But it cannot take away from us the human responsibility of choice and decision.

NOTES

1. In this respect, see my article "Preliminary Remarks on the Interaction Between American and European Social Science," *Social Research*, vol. 43, n. 1, 1976, pp. 25–45.

2. See Richard Münch, "American and European Social Theory: Cultural Identities and Social Forms of Theory Production," *Sociological Perspectives*, vol. 34, 1991, pp. 313–35.

3. In this respect, see my article in the journal edited by Giuseppe Semerari, "Sociologia e filosofia oggi," *Paradigmi*, vol. 3, n. 13, Jan.–April 1987, pp. 5–18.

4. See C. P. Snow, *The Two Cultures and the Scientific Revolution*, Cambridge, Eng.: Cambridge Univ. Press, 1959.

5. See R. E. Lane, "The Decline of Politics and Ideology in a Knowledgeable Society," *American Sociological Review*, n. 31, 1966, pp. 649–62. See also D. Bell, *The*

Coming of Post-Industrial Society, New York: Basic Books, 1973, and A. W. Gouldner, *The Future of Intellectuals and the Rise of the New Class*, New York: Seabury
Press, 1979.

    6. See J. Habermas, *The Theory of Communicative Action*, trans. by J. McCarthy,
Boston: Beacon Press, 1984, and A. Touraine, *Production de la société*, Paris: Seuil,
1985.

1

✛

Adam Ferguson: The Theory of "Civil Society"

THE SCOTTISH CONTEXT

I am trying to imagine what Scotland was like at the time of Adam Ferguson, in the last two-thirds of the eighteenth century. There are moments of grace in the life of countries and regions, just as in that of individuals. The Scotland of Ferguson is also the Scotland of Adam Smith, of John Millar, and of what is commonly called "the Scottish school," interested in considering the structural characteristics, psychological attitudes, and values of an evolving, mobile society, open to commerce but also to reflection on itself; trusting in science, but not thereby bound to scientific dogmatism. Perhaps already in the Scottish countryside there is, if not a precise metaphor, an idea of the judicious, pragmatic minimizing which in itself tempts so much of the English Enlightenment—a countryside which cannot be called monotonous, but which is not dramatic, varied enough to stimulate the imagination but also to console it.

What is most striking is the way in which a society can, little by little, become "laicized," withdrawing itself from the dead hand of the past and its conventions—without having in this process to undergo lacerations which are too deep and painful—basically without strain. Primary human groups cut out for themselves ever-wider areas of relative autonomy as regards State institutions and ecclesiastical structures. There thus was born a network of subinstitutional relations, which in their daily concrete unraveling make up the real sociological flesh of the institutional frameworks described and laid down by normative juridical formalism. Those relations assume importance only to the degree in which the whole of social life is not absorbed and, as it were, "consumed" by the spheres of official power—it matters little whether by princely power or by church power. In fact, we are dealing with relations which for the most part concern the material problems of life, the conditions of development and perpetuation of the community, commercial exchange, but also exchanges of culture, neighborhood, kinship, and friendship. What these relations cannot determine—indeed, what is removed from them in principle—are the major decisions on which the life of the community depends: that is to say, the decisions of war and peace.

Once upon a time, in that kind of society which Herbert Spencer was to call "military," counterposing it schematically to "industrial" society, all the activity of the community joined in and received its own justification from the state of war, actual or potential, which it had to face. In this perspective, the individual and the primary group to which he belonged were not basic values but rather subordinate to the imperatives of central power—or, more precisely, of the various power structures struggling one against the other. The modern era, in England and Scotland in the eighteenth century, was announced by the lessening of this subordination and the emergence of that dense network of relationships of both friendship and interest, very sensitive to specific local conditions, which as a whole is described as "civil society" to differentiate it from political society in the sense of "State" society or power in the strict sense, and from religious or hierocratic society in the formal sense.

It is to Adam Ferguson that we owe the first attempt to lay this new historical and social formation on a systematic theoretical basis. Ferguson was the son of a minister and himself (more than anything, to please his father) an ecclesiastic and student of theology for some time in Edinburgh University, and then, for about ten years, chaplain to the Black Watch. He eventually left the Church and was able to crown the dream of his life by becoming professor of moral philosophy at Edinburgh University.

BEYOND THE *BELLUM OMNIUM CONTRA OMNES* ("THE WAR OF EACH AGAINST ALL")

"Civil society" is, for Ferguson, the confirmation, historical as well as logical, that "the war of plunder or defense" cannot be the basic, founding aim of human groups associated in society. The outlook of Ferguson's reasoning is clearly directed against the idea of the *bellum omnium contra omnes* of Hobbes. Indeed, "if the war of plunder and defense were the principal aim of nations, every tribe from its first stage would aspire to the condition of a Tartar horde, and in all its successes would hasten to achieve the greatness of a Tartar Empire. The military leader would take

the position of the Civil Magistrate, and concerns for the necessary prepa-
rations to flee with all possessions or to set off with all its forces would, in
every society, represent the whole of public provisions."[1]

Ferguson's observation, as reordered here, may appear convincing.
However, it should be noted that while in general the anti-Hobbesian
positions are discussed on the basis of characteristically Aristotelian
considerations of the logico-deductivist kind—whereby it is rare that
they avoid falling into crude logical inversions or mere tautologies (for
example, by deriving the existence of society from the definition of man
as "a being social by nature"—while it is precisely this characteristic of
"sociability" or "sociality" which should be explained. Even so, Ferguson is too alert not to be aware of the fragility of explanatory reasonings
whose basis does not go beyond a totality of presuppositions, however
logical, to be elaborated.

Therefore he refers to historical proof, by setting out a series of historical exemplifications which in his view will enable us to understand how
the very phenomenon of a war (of which Ferguson is very careful not to
deny the importance, both as an internal and an external fact, to the nation) obeys in reality a logic which transcends it and gives it a precise
function, but only in situations of emergency. If it were not thus, Ferguson
somewhat rhetorically asks—and it is clear that here there reappears, and
makes itself heard, the habit of sermonizing—how would the names and
undertakings of Licurgus or Solon, supreme legislators, be transmitted to
the memory and praise of posterity? We would have had to have been
content with the exploits of Hercules or Jason. Moreover, Ferguson continues, even the most warlike barbarian tribes, while they appear as ban-
dits to those on the outside, maintain within themselves "the strongest
sentiments of affection and honor."

The warlike drive is not, therefore, denied by Ferguson, as he is convinced that this would be equivalent to denying the evidence. Rather, it
should be placed in a wider context and to some extent reevaluated as an
activity in the service of civil society. In fact, it is here that one measures
the level of progress achieved by human groups. Ferguson states that it is
in the dispatching of the affairs of civil society that men find the exercise
of their best talents, as the objects of their best sentiments.[2] Further, it is in
its grafting onto the advantages of civil society that the art of war is per-
fected and the resources and complicated mechanisms on which the conduct of armies depend can be better understood.[3] We are far from what
were to be the ingenuous schemas of Spencer and Kant. At the same time,
it seems that in Ferguson's argument there is a breach with respect to the
most immediate problematic of "total war"—that is, a type of war which
not only concerns professional soldiers and professionals in the army, but
rather the whole population. However, civil society—and on this point

Ferguson is very clear—needs peace. The problem is, however, how to guarantee it? Where does peace derive its origin? Where is its basis?

THE RESTRAINT OF THE LAW

This is a classic concern of philosophical and social thought, which in modern times brings together words and styles of conceptual activity as different as those of Kant and Veblen.[4] Ferguson's response may seem almost disarmingly candid: "where men enjoy peace, they are indebted either to their mutual affections and considerations or to the restraints of the law."[5] Once again, however, the Scottish thinker does not desert his norm of robust, even prosaic, realism. One cannot take much account of the affections, even if it is clear that this would be the ideal path. One must have the "restraint" of law.

Here too, the modernity of Ferguson's thought is striking. He does not set off seeking a mythical "natural law," a prime foundation of the most ancient, divine origin, according to the hypotheses of Plato (in *The Laws*), so swiftly taken up and transformed into a dogma by Greco-Latin patristics and systematically developed by natural law theory up to Passerin d'Entreves and Leo Strauss.[6] The historical and essentially "conventional" nature of laws—typical group decisions to be operated with regard to, and eventually also against, individual options when these endanger the stability and future of the community—does not escape him. He said, "law is a convention on which members of a particular community have found agreement and on the basis of which both the Magistrate and the subject continue to enjoy their rights and to maintain the peace of society."[7] We might deduce that in Ferguson we have the pure representative of juridical nominalism, but this conclusion would appear hasty to any long, nonsuperficial examination of his position. In fact, the aim of law lies in preserving the conditions of peace in society. The cause of disturbance of these conditions is to be sought, according to Ferguson, in the *auri sacra fames*, or a desire for immoderate gain, tendentially harmful to the interests of others, with the aim of increasing individual (personal) private property.[8]

Ferguson thus manages to outline not only a vague cluster of tendencies or psychological inclinations, nor does he stop at the formal logic of a purely juridical reasoning. Here he touches upon a structural element of modern society, its fundamental stratifying principle on the basis of which society itself is dichotomously divided into what Marx and Engels were to call in the *Manifesto* the "two enemy camps": those who possess and those who are possessed by *private property*. Ferguson explains that the desire for profit is the great source of injustices. The law has, therefore, an essential relationship with property. It must determine the various methods whereby property can be acquired as in prescription by convention and by succession, and take the necessary steps to make possession of property secure.

According to Ferguson, therefore, laws exist as conventions tending to protect and make secure possession and enjoyment of private property. The importance of the latter is beyond discussion, and one understands the admiration which Marx and Engels had for Ferguson, even if the social consequences which they drew from the crucial function of private property radically diverged from those specified by Ferguson. The latter does not think in terms of relations of production, and still less manages to state theoretically the existence and dynamic complexity of social classes based on exploitation on the one hand, and alienation on the other. However, in his work there is no shortage of dazzling intuitions which, even in a still moralizing tone, do, nonetheless, bear an unmistakable pre-Marxian accent and at the same time a clearly anti-Utopian and anti-Rousseauian orientation. The idea—so fruitful for the social sciences—here emerges that the individual, convinced that he moves and acts for his immediate advantage, in reality obeys a broader and more complex design. As in the case of the "invisible hand" of his fellow countryman, Adam Smith, which is supposed to guide individuals unbeknownst toward betterment—so that the search for the satisfaction of individual egoisms is supposed inevitably to end up in collective happiness—so, too, Ferguson's individuals, animated by their thirst for profit and affection toward their future heirs, work, without knowing it, for the construction of civil society. Ferguson argues: "Men, in following the present sentiment of their minds, driving themselves to remove difficulties or to achieve manifest and graspable advantages, arrive at results which not even their imagination would have been able to foresee, and, like other living beings, proceed in the path of their nature without perceiving its end. He who first said 'I want to acquire this field; I will leave it to my heirs' did not at all suppose that he was laying down the bases of civil laws and political institutions. He who first submitted to a leader did not understand that he was giving an example of fixed subordination which for the greedy men would be a pretext for taking over his possessions, and for an arrogant man, a pretext for requiring his service."[9]

MAN AS A NATURALLY AND HISTORICALLY SOCIAL BEING

In comparison with Rousseau, Ferguson's text provides a measure of the distance between the world of English Enlightenment and that of French pre-Revolutionary thought. Also to be noted is the psychological identification of social behavior (greed, arrogance) which, however, is never such that the outlines and structural characteristics of important social phenomena are lost to view. What interests us chiefly is the awareness of the "heterogenesis of ends." A lay providence seems to watch over the destinies of humanity. What at first sight—as with war—appears to be a destructive phenomenon in reality makes necessary a series of social provisions which in the medium-term appear as decisive for the construction of the community, especially in the aspects of its civil, nonwarlike, life. The thirst for profit, which is the origin of injustice and private property itself—that is to say, the least ambiguous in that it can express affection for heirs and kin, but also greediness and arrogance toward subordinates—is then the opportunity for the promulgation of laws which can safeguard the life of the community as a group. They become the channels and privileged instruments for the historic realization of civil society.

Man is, in fact, not adapted to a solitary life. It is not by returning to the forest or an ill-defined "state of nature" that man finds conditions for his improvement and progress. He needs his neighbor. He needs the affection of those close to him but also paradoxically, their rivalry. Ferguson writes that "without rivalry between nations and the practice of war, civil society itself would have had difficulty in finding an end or a form. Man would have been able to establish relationships without formal conventions, but they would never have been able to live in security without a national argument."[10] What is true for war is also true for private property.

The phenomenon which Veblen was to describe with ruthless precision as "invidious comparison" and which can poison interpersonal relationships between neighbors and members of the same community, is brought out by Ferguson in its positive aspects. Indeed, he sees deriving from this the social function of private property, that amount of rational and calculated foresight which is necessarily required by any process of enrichment, those virtues of hard work and saving which are at the basis of the primitive accumulation of capital, both private and personal as well as social, and which it is not enough to deride as moralistic attitudes or products to believe one has adequately explained them.[11]

Ferguson's description is, in my view, a small masterpiece of phenomenological analysis in which the psychological level confronts and interacts with the structural level in an extraordinarily complex evolutionary framework. "As soon as a parent begins to desire for his own children a better provision than that which they find through an equal sharing out between many members, and as soon as he has used his labor and skill separately, he tends towards exclusive possession and looks for ownership of the land as well as the enjoyment of his products. When the individual no longer finds among his fellows the same inclination to put everything in common for public use, he falls prey to concern for his personal fortune. He is alarmed by the solicitude for themselves which everyone else demonstrates, and is moved as much by emulation and jealousy as by the sense of necessity. He then accepts that considerations for his own interest should sprout in his mind, and that when immediate need is satisfied he can also act in the light of the future, or rather find an aim for his vanity in amassing those things which have become the object of competition and matters of general esteem. Driven on by this motivation, when the paths of violence are closed to him, he can apply his activity to lucrative skills to bear the weight of a tedious task and to await the result of his labor with patience, which requires time. Thus men acquire industry through many slow degrees. They are taught to consider their own interest, to abstain from illegitimate profits. They are guaranteed in the possession of what they honestly pursue. It is by these means that gradually the habits of the laborer, the artisan, and the trader are formed."[12]

THE INTEGRATION OF NATURE AND CULTURE

"Nature" and "culture" are thus not counterpoised in Ferguson but rather mutually integrate and aid each other. The problem of whether the sociality of man is natural or, instead, historically acquired would probably have seemed to him an idle question. Faced with the demand, he would have replied: "It is always in groups and societies that men have wandered or fixed stable dwellings, made conventions or fought. The cause of their being found together, whatever it may be, is the principle of their alliance or union."[13] Ferguson understands at once how the problem of coexistence is badly put in Rousseau: by starting from the individual, it is no longer possible to arrive at society. Moreover, the problems of the individual are not an individual fact. He quotes Montesquieu: man is born in society and there he stays. How is this?

Here, once again, the good luck of a primary socialization which was peculiarly happy and without disturbances probably makes its weight felt. It is not by chance that Ferguson mentions in the first place "the affection for parents who, instead of abandoning the adult man as happens among animals, bind him to them even closer to the extent in which to this initial sentiment are united the esteem and remembrance of its first effects."[14] This "affection for parents" could seem less true today than yesterday, bearing in mind the endemic crisis in which the family connection finds itself today, even in those cultures in which it seemed destined to remain indefinitely the mainstay and secret shock absorber. However, it is hard not to see also in Ferguson's phrases the echo of unforgettable existential experiences: the peaceful tread and serenity of certain Sunday walks with his father, hand in hand, on the green and yellow crags of the Highlands.

In fact, Ferguson sees in loneliness an irremedial evil: "Sadness and melancholy are tied to loneliness, and tenderness and pleasure to relationships among men. A solitary navigator discovers with joy the traces of a Laplander on the snow-covered shore."[15] The evidence on which Ferguson tends to base his certainties almost always refers back to common sense or historical experience. At any rate, he turns away from, distrusts, the typical schemas of evolutionistic mechanicism, which of necessity postulates a basic continuity between the realm of minerals, vegetables, animals, and the human world. At the same time, however, with equal clarity, he criticizes the hedonistic hypothesis. Men do not live as isolated beings, not only and not so much because like certain families of animals they gather together as a herd, ready to follow naturally and unreflectingly the group of their own species. Nor, according to Ferguson, is it possible conclusively to demonstrate that the mainspring of every social action, and the very formation of the community, should have its roots in individual advantage or fear and thus in the necessity of defense and protection.

Instead, Ferguson comes back to insist on the importance of affection. What he calls the "intentional perspectives of interest" should not be excluded but are not by themselves sufficient to explain the genesis and existence of society. The advantages which "men draw from commerce and reciprocal aid" are not enough. One must dig deeper. Further, one must not lose sight of the problem, which is not that of social productivity, nor that of security of the individual, nor of the group seen by itself. The question to which one must respond concerns the fact of the social order, of the how and why "men stay together."

SOCIETY AS A GLOBAL, HISTORICAL, THAT IS, PROBLEMATICALLY OPEN, STRUCTURE

Undoubtedly, society is a fact of "togetherness," a phenomenon of belonging. Students of social problems, especially contemporary ones, have long been mesmerized, if not obsessed, by problems of social change and revolutions. They have wrongly assumed the social order to be a datum taken for granted as an acquired result no longer worthy either of reflection or of critical analysis. Ferguson's remarks in this regard are of extraordinary immediate interest. The social order can never be taken for granted. It is forever to be rediscovered and remade. There is no society which is not a daily reinvention. The institutional complexes, which might be limited to repeating themselves with monotonous everyday cadences, run the risk of cutting out the emotional tie which binds them to the real social process, which is vitally fluid, and they would end up dried out, dead, lifeless as empty husks.

Society is a "togetherness" but not given once and for all, nor mechanically comparable to a mere juxtaposition, nor dogmatically predictable as regards its developments. It is a "togetherness"—that is, a global historical structure—which is problematically open and relatively indeterminate, in which natural aptitudes and conscious decisions, material interests and affective ties, motivations and values, are intermingled. Ferguson argues, "Neither an inclination of men to join together as a herd, nor the consideration of the advantages linked to this condition, include all the principles by which men have remained together. These links are only weak in structure if they are compared to the burning enthusiasm with which a man attaches himself to his friend, his tribe, or those with whom he has at times travelled along the road of destiny. The reciprocal discoveries of generosity and the common tests of courage reinforce the enthusiasm for friendship. They arouse an enthusiasm in the human heart which cannot be suppressed by considerations of interest or by thought for personal security."[16] The ties of affection and friendship are exalted by Ferguson as the basic factors which hold the human community together. He concludes: "From this source are derived not only the strength but the very existence of his most felicitous emotions. . . . Send him [man] into a desert where he lives alone: he is a plant torn off from its roots. The form may yet be preserved, but every faculty declines and withers. The human character and personality cease to exist."[17]

It is in this deep constructive need of interpersonal relations that Ferguson grasps the qualitative difference, the real leap between the animal world and human society. Furthermore, here his break with any scheme of ingenuous, more or less markedly historical, evolutionism becomes obvious. However, the contrast involves not only classical evolutionism. An even greater one is opened up between Ferguson and the most recent ethological approaches.[18] According to Ferguson, "We are forced to observe that men have always presented themselves as a distinct and superior species among animals, and that neither the possession of similar organs, nor the resemblance of form, nor the use of the hand, nor the continuity of the relationship with this sovereign artist, have ever rendered other species able to confuse their nature or their inventions with that of man; and that in his crudest state he finds himself above other animals; and that even in his most extreme degradation he never descends to their level."[19]

Ferguson's reference to the "sovereign artist" may, for instance, make us fear for a moment a commonplace lapse into the spiritualist or idealist rhetoric which seems a basic characteristic of the old humanism, especially where Ferguson states that "we can learn nothing about the nature of man from the analogy with other animals."[20] In reality, it seems to me that Ferguson escapes the typical deficiencies of spiritualist and idealist outlooks, thanks both to his rejection of a meta-historical natural law basis, and to his constant referral, instead, to historical evidence as it emerges from research and meditation. The presence of man in historically known time signifies for Ferguson an essential integration between nature and culture, so that it does not appear possible—save analytically and conventionally—to separate art and nature, the original biogenetic endowment from the maturation of intelligence and awareness. He says "We speak of art as distinct from nature; but art is itself natural to man."[21] Further on, with greater clarity: "If, therefore, we are asked where the state of nature could be found, we could reply: It is here, and it doesn't matter if we mean to refer to the island of Great Britain, the Cape of Good Hope, or the Straits of Magellan."[22]

NOTES

1. A. Ferguson, *An Essay on the History of Civil Society* [1767], Edinburgh: Edinburgh Univ. Press, 1966; cited from the Italian tran.: *Saggio sulla storia società*, Firenze: Vallecchi, 1973, p. 176. (*Note*: Throughout, all English translations of cited material are mine.)

2. Ferguson, *An Essay on the History of Civil Society*, p. 177.

3. Ferguson, *An Essay on the History of Civil Society*, p. 177.

4. Cf. I. Kant, *Zum ewigen Friede* (English tran.: *Principles of Lawful Politics*, trans. by W. Schwarz, Aalen, Denmark: Scientia, 1988); Thorstein Veblen, *Inquiry into the Nature of Peace and the Terms of its Perpetuation*, New York: Macmillan, 1917. The same concern is present in Saint-Simon: cf. *Oeuvres*, vol. 1., Paris: Anthropos, 1966, chap. 3, "Examen de la paix perpétuelle," pp. 1766 ff.

5. Ferguson, *An Essay on the History of Civil Society*, p. 177.

6. Cf. Leo Strauss, *Natural Right and History*, Chicago: Univ. of Chicago Press, 1953.

7. Ferguson, *An Essay on the History of Civil Society*, p. 178.

8. Ferguson, *An Essay on the History of Civil Society*, p. 178.

9. Ferguson, *An Essay on the History of Civil Society*, p. 141.

10. Ferguson, *An Essay on the History of Civil Society*, p. 31.

11. See in this respect Schumpeter's remarks on Marx and Engels's attitude toward the birth of capitalism and the function of saving: J. A. Schumpeter, *Capitalism, Socialism and Democracy*, New York: Harper & Bros., 1942.

12. Ferguson, *An Essay on the History of Civil Society*, p. 113.

13. Ferguson, *An Essay on the History of Civil Society*, p. 21.

14. Ferguson, *An Essay on the History of Civil Society*, p. 22.

15. Ferguson, *An Essay on the History of Civil Society*, p. 22.

16. Ferguson, *An Essay on the History of Civil Society*, p. 23.

17. Ferguson, *An Essay on the History of Civil Society*, p. 24.

18. Cf., for an overall view of the problems of ethology, G. De Crescenzo, *L'etologia e l'uomo*, Firenze: Nuova Italia, 1975. For some basic premises of ethology, K. Lorenz's *Taxis und Instinkthandlung in der Eirolbewegung des Graugans*, 1938, is indispensable—now in *Über tierisches und menschliches Verhalten*, Munich, 1965 (English tran.: *Studies in Animal and Human Behaviour*, trans. by R. Martin, Cambridge, Mass.: Harvard Univ. Press, 1970–71); see also his *On Aggression*, trans. by M. Kerr Wilson, New York: Harcourt, Brace & World, 1966, and *Instinct*, Princeton: Princetown Univ. Press, 1961. For a series of brilliant and partly ironic observations on the discussion, see J. Borges, *Discusión*, Buenos Aires: M. Gleizer, 1932 (Italian trans.: *Discussione*, trans. by L. B. Wilcock, Milano: Rizzoli, 1973, pp. 11–15).

19. Ferguson, *An Essay on the History of Civil Society*, p. 18.

20. On the superiority of men, see also the comments of Saint-Simon, *Oeuvres*, vol. 1, chap. 3.

21. Ferguson, *An Essay on the History of Civil Society*, p. 8.

22. Ferguson, *An Essay on the History of Civil Society*, p. 10.

2

✛

Claude-Henri de Saint-Simon: The Organic Nature of Society and the Possibility of Planning the Social Process

A MAN REPRESENTATIVE OF
THE CONTRADICTORINESS OF AN EPOCH

Aristocrat, revolutionary, inventor, industrialist, speculator and scientist, tireless traveler and passionate reformer to the limits of mysticism, socialist but also egocentric to the point of narcissism; Saint-Simon's life makes us think more of the vicissitudes of a Balzac character than of the life of a scholar of society. This should not be immensely surprising. In ages of rapid transition, when entire ideal universes, economic structures consolidated through the centuries and political regimes, orders, concepts, unexpectedly seem to drop into a state of accelerated transformation and the lived seems to be infinitely richer than the thought, there emerge on the historic horizon representative men who embody this instability in their very own passions and their whole destiny, thus uniting individual biography and historic-social structure. Two-faced Januses, they remind us of the past but at the same time anticipate the future. Within the tumultuous and often ambiguous events of their existential experience, they live the contradictory and lacerated nature of their time. "Inventors" dominated by Ulysses' complex, dissatisfied and perpetually wandering from idea to idea, from continent to continent, they sum up within the relatively short span of a single biography many lives, as if they touched and moved, in a schizophrenic way, on manifold levels, tending to embody and illuminate an entire age and its *Zeitgeist*.[1]

Saint-Simon is one of these extraordinary "representative men," first of all for his blending of thought and action. In Saint-Simon there is an acknowledged gap between *vita activa* and *vita contemplativa*, or, in other words, between theory and praxis. With him begins the experience of thinking as acting, or the discovery of the practical nature of thought. We can understand the explicit sympathy with him which Marx and Engels expressed—two characters who were certainly not tender-minded and in any case little inclined to recognize intellectual debts toward anyone. Second, Saint-Simon's representativeness is linked to the intuition, which was most lively in him, regarding the social importance of science, particularly of the socializing effects of scientific judgment, inasmuch as it is "stipulated" and intersubjective, about the nature and trends of the social process. Third, Saint-Simon anticipates modern industrial societies with his idea of the possibility of planning rationally—and therefore from the center—the whole economic and social life, from the point of view of a global transformation, or a psychological-moral and at the same time structural one, of the existing society.

For this purpose, traditional philosophy is no longer of any use. The politics inherited from the past and managed as a family affair concerns only restricted elites; it has reduced itself to a question of castes; it has lost any basic legitimacy; it keeps on its feet only by force of inertia. On the other hand, the revolutionary criticism has no positive operative abilities. It cannot start a rational reconstruction of the social order. Its critical ability is corrosive but its positive proposals are inadequate. It raises aims which are noble and collective, but indeterminate. It destroys the dogmas and the false certainties of the past but "humanity is not made for dwelling among ruins." The historical task which Saint-Simon assigns himself is the reorganization upon rational bases of European society though organic social reforms, scientifically guaranteed. What distinguishes him sharply from other social reformers is his awareness that the primary necessity before starting the work of reform is to put in hand the elaboration of a plan based on an accurate analysis and on a scientific exploration of the nature of society, of the historical form of the social processes and of the logic of their dynamic development. Furthermore Saint-Simon tries to single out which are the new emerging actors in the social process, the guiding forces of a modern society which is undergoing a process of industrialization. With an exceptional prophetic capacity, Saint-Simon sees in scientist-technicians—that is, in "industrialists" conceived not so much as proprietors and capital managers but rather as the regulators and functional supervisors of technical progress meant as the necessary result of scientific knowledge applied to production—the new protagonists, the new power class. In this sense, Saint-Simon is the first theorist of the industrial as well as of the so-called postindustrial society, in which scientific knowledge, more than proprietary rights, seems to be decisive. This will not prove very encouraging for many modern sociologists. They are arriving about two hundred years late.

SCIENTIFIC KNOWLEDGE AS A SOCIAL NEED

The guiding thread of Saint-Simon's social thought is provided by the need to know, scientifically speaking that is, as a matter of fact, on empirical bases, to tie, organize, reconstruct, recompose as a structure what lies scattered and fragmented. A post-Revolution man, he feels deeply and expresses with extraordinary eloquence the need to reconstruct institutions after the revolutionary earthquake. The Revolution taught him that even the most venerable and ancient institutions are in reality unprotected and weak. They may be attacked and overthrown. The social world presents none of the characteristic rigidities of the natural world, which, after every emergency, comes back to conditions of stability and normality— that is, to the initial condition. Nature is substantially unmodifiable. Society is by definition plastic. It is sufficient to have at one's disposal an aim, elaborate a plan, set up an operative project.

Lenin's admiration for Saint-Simon should not astonish us, aside from Marx and Engels. It is rare to find in a scholar of social problems of his period such an acute and precise awareness of the importance of the organizational instrument. Saint-Simon speaks and argues like a modern high-level "manager"—that is, like one of Galbraith's techno-structural managers. But whereas Galbraith's techno-structural manager discharges his function and his own self-image in the control of the internal operations of the organizational machine, having as his supreme standard the level of operative efficiency, independently of the broadest social repercussions outside the enterprises, Saint-Simon's industrial manager always faces problems which involve society as a global reality. "The philosophy of the last century has been revolutionary", states Saint-Simon. "That of the nineteenth century must be *organizing*. The lack of institutions leads to the destruction of any society: the old institutions extend the ignorance and the prejudices of the time in which they were created. Shall we be forced to choose between barbarism and stupidity?"[2]

This dilemma permeates all Saint-Simon's work. The answer is characteristically intellectualistic. The solution is sought in the intellectual clarity which is supposed to be by itself the resolution of the problem of the age. Here is already encapsulated, in a very abbreviated form, Auguste Comte's thesis on the "intellectual evil," that is, on the dependence of social crisis, in its widest meaning, on a deficient scientific understanding of the problems of society in their double aspect, both static and dynamic.

Saint-Simon directly calls intellectuals to account, underlines harshly the responsibilities which, on the basis of their own notion of knowledge as an operative fact, also in a practical sense, cannot ever be merely intellectual or moral, but also practical and political. "Writers of the nineteenth century," he pronounces, "it is up to you only to relieve us from this sad dilemma. The social order has been turned upside down, because it was no longer adapted to the new awarenesses [*aux lumières*]: it is up to you to rebuild it."[3] Saint-Simon is perfectly aware of the novelty and originality of his proposals.

He also knows that it is useless to pour new wine into old bottles and that minor, petty reformism has had its day. "For a long time," he writes with impressive lucidity, "we have agreed in saying that the political system is destroyed at its foundation and that it is necessary to establish another one; nevertheless, neither this generally widespread view nor the spirits prepared by the moil and toil of revolutions and wars to seize greedily upon all means to restore order and repose, have caused anyone to get out of the old routine; we dragged ourselves along with the old principles, as if there could not be better ones; the elements of the old system have been combined in a thousand ways; but nothing new has been conceived. The plan of organization that I have set forth is the first that might have a new and general character."[4]

PLANNING AS A CONDITION OF SOCIAL PROGRESS

Saint-Simon's "plan" is based on a conception of the social process which views it as an organic whole of functions and as an absolute rational structure. That in fact the social process appears to be traversed by crisis and broken up by contradictions is due, according to Saint-Simon, to the ignorance, the consolidated and egoistic interests linked to tradition, to old habits—in a word: to irrationality.

Saint-Simon is ready to acknowledge that, as regards the specific contents, his plan may also not be good or may even be conceived as essentially bad [*essentiellement mauvais*]. All this seems to him to be of secondary importance. What instead appears basic to him is that a "plan" be nonetheless elaborated and be thus put into practice. What seems to him to be deeply erroneous and ultimately absurd is that one might go on abandoning social life into the hands of chance, subjected to the contradictory and negative pressure of particular interests, oriented not by reasoning but, in the best hypothesis, by pure and simple habits. In this sense it is difficult to deny Saint-Simon the paternity of the vast modern movement of opinion which is economic but also sociopolitical, anthropological and generally cultural, concerned with the possibility of programming the economic choices and of planning, as a whole and on an even planetary scale, social life.[5]

Perhaps here, more than in other aspects of the essentially "seminal" thought of this pioneer, we can trace the roots of his modernity. Undoubtedly Marx and Engels admired the clarity with which Saint-Simon outlines the situation of those whom he defines as the "modern slaves," that is, the employees in those industries which appear to him as "enemies of pacific industry." We have not yet got to the conception of the worker who offers his labor power in a formally free market, one of the fundamental conditions, according to Max Weber, for the rise of modern capitalism. But we are striding toward it.[6] However, even more explicit and suggestive is the perception Saint-Simon offers as regards the rationalization of social life and especially "rationality as regards the end," or what Max Weber was to call *Zweckrationalität*. Above all, it is striking that Saint-Simon did not allow himself to become trapped by the differentiation and eventual contradictoriness of specific contents but, on the contrary, limited himself to the consideration of the form of collective action orientated to an aim. What matters, as he makes very clear in "Industry," is the sense of forming a *ligue*, as it were, a conglomeration of converging wills, a Bund, the result of *idem velle atque nolle*, as he emphasizes, quoting Sallust. The process of rationalization cannot therefore be defined on the grounds of determinate contents, which of course may vary even substantially. It is defined as a way of acting, and organizing the available resources toward objective considered as desirable. "The league is the union of effort," Saint-Simon explains. "Everywhere there is an objective towards which men tend by mutual consent [*de concert*]; there, and only there, a nation exists."[7]

Here I think we are at a safe distance from the conception, still very romantic, of the *homme de génie*, or super-man, to which Saint-Simon seemed to be tied in his early works, especially in the *Lettres d'un habitant de Genève*. The scientific process is essentially an impersonal one which can leave out or even turn against individual options or whims. It must nevertheless be considered Saint-Simon's brilliant intuition as regards the correlation between creativity and marginality. "Run through the history of the progressions of the human spirit," he writes, "and you will see that almost all masterpieces are owed to isolated and often persecuted men. Once they have been nominated academicians, they are almost always asleep in their armchairs."[8] But what is true for the constitution of the "nation" is even more true for the foundation of any society: "Any system of society . . . has as its definite aim that of moving towards an objective of activity all specific force. For there is no society except where there is *a general and combined action* [*une action générale et combinée*]."[9]

SOCIETY AS ORGANIZATIONAL FACT AND
THE "SCIENTIFICATION" OF POLITICAL DECISIONS

The formative action of any human society is an organized one, continuous through time, directed toward an explicit objective, coordinated in its various aspects and organized as to the necessary means to achieve the predetermined aim. It is on the grounds of this basic criterion of judgment that Saint-Simon evaluates the political action of his time and finds it irremediably lacking, still feudal, tied to unjustifiable prerational traditions, slow and confused, incapable of serving the purposes which it proposes and of satisfying, totally and immediately, historically emerging social and individual demands. It is necessary, in the first place, according to Saint-Simon, to reorganize political action so as rationally to reorient and found scientifically European society. Where are the forces capable of undertaking and carrying out this enterprise? Who will be the protagonists of this true, substantial revolution?

We have earlier noticed Saint-Simon's peculiar predictions concerning "modern slavery," which foreshadow the Marxist idea of the subaltern working classes, forced to sell their labor power, or *Arbeitskraft*, to survive and therefore to let themselves be "owned" by the means of production and their proprietors, just as we have emphasized the wholly Weberian modernity of his notion of "rationality as regards the aim." Equally remarkable is Saint-Simon's insistence on the "organizational" instrument and its socially decisive importance, which reminds us of Lenin, and his identification in the "industrialists," in the specific sense of "industrial operators," that is, of functional controllers (not only juridical ones) of the productive apparatus—the decisive forces of modern industrial society which foretell modern theorizations of the "technostructure" and generally technocracy.

Saint-Simon is convinced that first of all it is necessary to find "a new system of political organization." Politics and the traditional politicians appear to him to be deprived of any binding meaning and devoid at the same time of any operative ability. The reason is clear: current politics was perfectly adequate to achieve the objectives of a premodern feudal society; it is essentially incapable, that is, dysfunctional, as regards achieving the objectives of a modern industrial society, which are not wartime ventures or chivalric exploits, despite the increase in production by means of the application of scientific knowledge of the productive cycle.

In prerevolutionary feudal society it was perfectly legitimate that power should be in the hands of dynastic groups, born and bred for war; in the modern age, power must be acknowledged and given to those who are capable, through their personal abilities and their scientific knowledge, to serve the ends which define industrial society, that is, the organization of industrial production. It is upon the latter, and no longer upon wars, that the future and welfare of society depend. For this reason, Saint-Simon thinks that the old "parliaments" must be replaced by a new "industrial parliament," technically competent, scientifically able to organize and to make the productive apparatus work. In a word, *it is necessary to scientificize political decisions.*

Industrial production is therefore for Saint-Simon the universal mover. According to Jean-Baptiste Say's model, especially in his *Traité d'économie politique* (Paris, 1803), Saint-Simon effectively summarizes his position:

1) the production of useful goods constitutes the only reasonable and positive aim that political societies can propose for themselves, and therefore "respect production and producers," which is, according to Saint-Simon, a slogan to be preferred to the more usual one: "respect property and proprietors";
2) the government damages industry whenever it interferes in its internal affairs;
3) the producers of useful goods are the only people who are useful to society and therefore *the task of regulating its development is theirs alone*;
4) men cannot ever direct their forces against one another without damaging production; therefore, abolish wars;
5) the desire of a people to dominate another people is wrong because it implies the use of force and therefore a stoppage, and therefore decrease, of production;
6) parallel to production, morality also improves;
7) since the whole human species has a common aim and common interests, every man in his social relationships must be considered solely as employed in a work-team.

In short, for Saint-Simon politics is the science of production, or the science which has as its aim the order of things most favorable for all kinds of production.

From this summary it might be argued that Saint-Simon has no awareness of the fact that politics is in reality the science of power and at the same time the science, or the art, of the most opportune or favorable decisions for the individual, or the group, who takes it in a determinate situation. A suspicion of intellectualism is surely legitimate with regard to Saint-Simon's political conception, just like the constructions and proposals of all utopians. But in the case of Saint-Simon the suspicion mentioned above is only partially well-grounded. In fact he asks: "If this is as I think, the situation in which industry finds itself today in its political career, how is it that the management of *society* has not yet passed into its hands? How is it that the *preindustrial regime* continues to survive?"[10] First of all, in answering, Saint-Simon emphasizes the intellectual causes (little knowledge of the "industrial principles," therefore little credit, etc.); but then he touches on the fundamental reason: industry—in order to place itself at the head of society, as should be its right—must not only be abstractly correct in principle; there has to be "a means, and a legal means, to make *power* pass into its hands."[11] This "means" must be legal, because any insurrection or revolt, or revolutionary movement, would be contrary to the "interests of industry" which are essentially pacific, and which need normality for the regularity of their processes. The risk of an involution would be serious. There might recur, according to Saint-Simon, that which had already happened at the time of the 1789 French Revolution, when it was a question of simply taking note of the dissolution of the aristocratic, theological, and feudal regime, handing power over to industrialists and scientists, while in reality, owing to operational errors, power ended up in the hands of those whom Saint-Simon calls the "leaguers," who direct the Revolution with the "principles of metaphysics," that is to say, against itself.

Nevertheless, and in spite of all the difficulties interposed by the "military and feudal class," the progress of industry stands out as certain and unstoppable. If the word "industry" were replaced by the word "bourgeoisie" we would obtain in Saint-Simon the same triumphal hymn that Marx and Engels raise to the latter in the *Manifesto*. The progress which is noticed by Marx and Engels in terms of modernization of the feudal world and of the struggle against "the idiocy of rural life" are, on the contrary, regarded by Saint-Simon as victories against poverty in general and against the military class. We arrive at the paradox. "Thanks to a happy and necessary effect of the perfection of *military art*, war is increasingly dependent on *industry*, so much so that today the real *military power* has passed into the hands of the industrialists." Here is a connection which escaped even Herbert Spencer's meticulous attention!

It is necessary, therefore, to translate into political formulas this actual power. Saint-Simon now writes as the legitimator of industry, the newly emerging social power. He proposes the setting up of an "industrial Parliament." He views it as the crowning of "all the efforts that the civil nations have been making for the past six centuries and the aim of the great *European* revolution which has long been in preparation." It is strange how Saint-Simon has not a shadow of doubt that there is present, in his own scientific judgment, an element of indeterminacy sufficient to invalidate all his laborious construct. Political activity, as a specific one tending to gain increasingly significant amounts of power and therefore to legitimate both its possession and its practical exercise, seems to have remained basically external to Saint-Simon's reforming concerns. The idea, thus, that this might arise, apart form the "military" and "feudal" services, also to a "tyranny of progress," would have appeared to him only as a paradox or perhaps an intolerable absurdity. It is also odd that Saint-Simon, author of *Nouveau Christianisme*, did not realize the contradiction running between the "industrial regime," which he foretold, and the "religions of brotherhood." Be they intelligent, or "productive" or less so, the "religion of brotherhood" allows of no discrimination between its own members. A brother is always a brother. The brotherhood relationship does not admit selectivity; on the contrary, it denies it in principle. For this reason, there is a radical opposition between the religions of brotherhood and formally contractual and rationalist societies—that is, industrialized societies. It is almost incredible how this contradiction, which undoubtedly involves the "industrialist principle," completely escapes Saint-Simon who, on the contrary, theorizes the renewal of Christianity. This was not to escape Max Weber later on.

NOTES

1. See the incredible autobiographical evidence of Saint-Simon in *Oeuvres*, vol. 1, Paris: Anthropos, 1966, pp. 64–88. (E.g.: "I was the closest relative of a well known author, the Duc de Saint-Simon. His duchy, his estate in Spain and 500.000 livres in rent which he enjoyed passed over my head. He quarrelled with my father, who disinherited him. I thus lost the titles and fortune of the Duc de Saint-Simon, but I inherited his passion for glory" [p. 71].)
2. Saint-Simon, *Oeuvres*, vol. 1, p. 158.
3. Saint-Simon, *Oeuvres*, vol. 1, p. 158.
4. Saint-Simon, *Oeuvres*, vol. 1, p. 245.
5. On Saint-Simon's discussion of the processes of planning, but in turn conditioned by an interdependent world-order, see the interesting article by Nicolaus Sombart, "Planung und Planetarissierung," *Merkur*, n. 197, July 1964, pp. 601–14.
6. See Saint-Simon, *Oeuvres*, vol. 1, p. 116: "The same condition as was called slavery in antiquity is to be found today in modern states with all the details which constituted its nature. *Slavery* still exists, therefore. *Slavery* persists as in antiquity, but it is no longer the same type of man who is the *slave*. To be a slave means to live under the arbitrary power, in the heart of a society of men who live under the law. We know who were slaves under the ancients: they were tradesman and shopkeepers, all those who practiced peaceful industry. It is enough today to look around to see who the slaves are: they are the soldiers, all those who practise industry hostile to peaceful industry."
7. Saint-Simon, *Oeuvres*, vol. 2, p. 26.
8. Saint-Simon, *Oeuvres*, vol. 1, p. 16.
9. Saint-Simon, *Oeuvres*, vol. 4, p. 45.
10. Saint-Simon, *Oeuvres*, vol. 2, p. 158.
11. Saint-Simon, *Oeuvres*, vol. 2, p. 159.

3

✝

Karl Marx and Friedrich Engels: The Dynamics of the Social System

DIFFICULTIES OF INTERPRETATION

A thick covering of interpretations has grown up over Marxism. As a complex theory which incorporates and implies at least one philosophy, an economics and socio-anthropology, Marxism has inspired a series of hermeneutic efforts as abundant as they have been biased (in the sense that each commentator has understandably proposed to find in Marx, as though in a kind of ambiguous and bottomless mine, what most rewarded him). The difficulty of understanding Marxism at its core is not, however, to be attributed to Marx and Engels's work, which generally appears extraordinarily percipient and direct, given that it is at times devoted to proselytism. Rather, one should bear in mind the fact that Marxist thought is a powerfully interconnected and logically coherent whole, although it is also orientated along the lines of a rich variety of perspectives such as to make an overall view necessary in order to master its meaning and general progression. One should not, furthermore, forget an additional element of difficulty. Marxism is a conceptual construct, but also a political movement. It is a complex of terms and propositions, like any theory of society, but it is also the theoretical premise for practical political action which has been going on now for more than a century and which has experienced different emphases—even radically antithetical ones—according to the specific historical context and political characteristics of the social framework in which it has been realized. This latter characteristic of Marxim as a political movement should probably be considered responsible for the fact, seemingly inexplicable, which until recently denied Marx and Engels the right of citizenship in the approved texts of sociology, understood at its highest as science of society. Behind this "veto" lay not only, as the zealots of political immediacy claimed, a desire for political intolerance or the attempt to exclude from normal intellectual circles Marxian thought with its obvious revolutionary indications. There was also an epistemological and methodological approach in scientific research which today is superceded in its mechanistic aspects and those of crude naturalistic objectivism. In other words, there was also buried in that, the notion which is clearly acknowledged as untenable today: that science was a kind of "divine knowledge," capable of expanding necessary and necessitating "laws," timeless and metahistorical, absolutely valid for every epoch and every place. What was taken unfavorably as remarkable in Marxism—that is, the explicit assumption of a particular point of view, that of the working class as potential "general class"—now shines out as its historic value, not only in a directly political sense, but in fact from a cognitive and scientific point of view. What has to be brought out is that the adoption of the proletarian point of view does not involve translating the results of observation and scientific sociological analysis into instantaneous political terms. Rather, it means the conscious historical self-location of the analyst, who thus clarifies at the outset the value motives and premises of his or her work, the guiding hypotheses which give him or her direction, as distinct from specific research hypotheses, and the political value of the possible conclusions.

MARXISM AS A SOCIOLOGY OF THE SYSTEMATIC ERA

In this light, Marxism may justly be presented as one of the great sociologies of the systematic age.[1] I am calling those conceptual constructions which are the result of the reflection and research of an individual "grand individual" sociologies of the systematic era (in Marx's case one should never forget Engels's contribution, which in my view, especially as regards empirical research, was perhaps more significant than is ordinarily believed); that is, systems which emerge as self-consistent and global, or intended to account for a social system—viewed overall as rational conjuncture, and, for this reason, intelligible as regards the components which make it up and the dynamic tensions which give it direction and define the progress of its evolution. There is thus no question of picking out in Marx's complex thought a sociology, just as one might identify and specify in it a philosophy, an economics, an anthropology, a theology more or less eschatological or "Messianic." This work of paring down is not only condemned from the beginning to failure insofar as by cutting up what appears to be a unitary whole, the operation runs the risk of finding a corpse in its hands.[2] This can only give rise to misleading and negative interpretative effects, since what is characteristic of Marxism is lacking: its global and synoptic character; its ability to grasp the interconnections which really make up the social; its vision of the totality of the dialectical connections which hold together the components of a society and make it a whole—that is, a structure, living and growing. In my view, Marxism, by way of its typical quality of being a global system and dialectically open, cannot be read and interpreted as a classical sociology alongside the others. But indeed, from the start, and much more than other sociologies (even the classical ones), even though these are bound to the false notion of the "dominant factor," Marxism also contains a basic sociological element, in that sociology, among all the social sciences, is the one defined on the basis of its interdisciplinary and meta-specialistic character with the aim of exploring the social as such.

The danger of an analysis which, starting with this "general" and "synoptic" attitude, may finish up only by being generic and unfocused is in Marx cleverly avoided by taking up the proletarian point of view. In other words, Marxism arises from the synthesis at a high level of extraction which is nonetheless historically rooted, between the specific studies to which it gives rise and in which it works as a method, tied to the canons of historical materialism and the form of its own method which is macrosociologic and dialectical. In this sense, Marxism manages to be specific without being specialistic and it is dialectical without as a result becoming inevitably philosophizing.

THE HEURISTIC IMPORTANCE OF "POINT OF VIEW"

At this point, it should be sufficiently clear why, in my opinion, Marx should be considered one of the founding fathers of sociology, even though the "point of view" from which he starts and which is always held firmly as the premise of the analysis, is really political, or relates to a meta-theoretical choice. It should just be noted that the premises of Tocqueville or Comte or Spencer or even, if you wish, Machiavelli are similarly political. A close reading of Marx, just as a reading of the authors quoted and many others that one might quote, brings to our attention how much "point of view," clearly and not covertly taken for granted and elaborated, is productive not so much as a political prospectus, and related to possible political action to be undertaken, but rather as an instrument of analysis. Or, more precisely, as a value-assumption and thus a criterion of judgment, bearing in mind the ability for analysis, description, explanation, and prevision of social phenomena.

One scholar has observed that "Marxism and classical sociology are both reflections on capitalism and bourgeois society. Both in their own way express disappointment in the bourgeois revolution. . . . However, the similarities end here and are swamped by the differences. . . . There is not a single eminent sociologist in the capitalist world who has, as a sociologist, taken part in a militant movement of workers. . . . This basic distance between Marxism and academic sociology should be specially borne in mind now that Marxist ideas are the object of discussion among sociologists."[3]

These are well-founded observations, with which one may basically agree though with two important reservations. In the first place, academic sociology is not the only sociology possible. In the second place, one must avoid the reduction of the theoretical to the existential because of the risk this reduction involves of an essentially moralistic and psychologizing argument ad hominem. This would mean falling into a logically contradictory position, basically anti-Marxist.

For Marx and Engels, the assumption of the proletarian point of view involves a quite exact priority of analytic themes and instruments. As is commonly said, their research overturns the Hegelian idealistic approach and thus proceeds on the basis of the premises of historical dialectical materialism. It was Marx himself who conferred the plaudit of having put the Hegelian dialectic on its feet, "straightened out," when it had been walking on its head. However, Marxist materialism should not be confused either with the philosophical materialism of the classical tradition (Democritus) nor with that of the eighteenth century (D'Holbach, Helvetius, De La Mettrie, Eüchner). Nothing is further from Marx than an abstract discourse on the concept of matter or the essence of man or the world. Marxist materialism should rather be understood in terms of a "critical realism"; that is, as the need to consider the material relations of life into which those living in any historical epoch necessarily enter among themselves, as the basic point of departure—even if not an exclusive one—of any research concerning social phenomena.[4]

THE CONCEPT OF "STRUCTURE"

Always from an analytic point of view, that is, with reference to methodological instruments in the broad sense (by grasping both the concepts and the specific techniques used in the research), one must stress the particular dynamism of social facts which is continuously and logically brought out by Marx. One is not dealing with a vague evolutionistic tendency, which, after Herbert Spencer, is supposed to be characteristic of all reality from the mineral to the vegetable and finally the animal, man included. The dynamism Marx speaks of, and which emerges from his research on the capitalist system, refers rather to a real dialectical totality wherein the "reality" of the human and historical world cannot be perceived, still less explained on the basis of individual aspects or residues of the real. Rather, they can only be grasped in the complex of social relations and relations of production, in situating them in hard frontal contradiction in specific historically determined situations. Outside the dialectical whole and critical reflection on it, it is not possible to free oneself from "appearances" nor from "ideological false consciousness" which characterize both individual situations, isolated from their context and taken as they are, and the motives of individual historical agents.

Given these analytic premises, one can easily understand the importance of "structure" (*Struktur*) in Marxism. By this term, Marx means "the whole of relations of production," that is, "the real foundation on which rises a legal and political superstructure [*Überbau*] and to which correspond determinate forms of social consciousness."[5] These few lines, simple in appearance, have given rise to arguments of interpretation which are not yet finished. In Marx's text, the sentences which follow have not made interpretation simpler, but rather more complicated. "The mode of production of material life conditions the social, political and intellectual life process in general. It is not the consciousness of men that determines their being, but, on the contrary, their social being that determines their consciousness. . . . With the change of the economic foundation the entire immense superstructure is transformed more or less rapidly."[6]

Now, the problem which immediately presents itself is that of the relationship between "structure" and "superstructure." These two terms in Marx clearly indicate two levels analytically distinct, if not separate or differentiated by content, of reality, which are thus in mutual relations. What kind of relation are we dealing with?

In the quotation from Marx but also on the basis of the interpretation of many authoritative Marxists, this would appear to concern an asymmetrical relationship in which one should recognize the priority of the structure and an essentially derivative, or secondary, nature for the superstructure. There is no doubt that this interpretation was for many years dominant in Marxist circles, and that it has had a considerable part to play from the political point of view. It is sufficient to think of the whole of Marxism and the corresponding reformist policies of the period of the Second International, or the period of mechanistic or dialecticized Marxism, according to which communism was awaited as an almost automatic product of certain objective "structural" changes, convinced that everything else—that is, "superstrutural" modifications—would have arrived miraculously in addition as the inevitable consequence of those modifications.

THE RELATIVE AUTONOMY OF THE "SUPERSTRUCTURE"

In other words, one must accept that even many authoritative interpretations of Marxism have made gross errors by confusing the relationship of "conditioning" which Marx sets up between the two levels, summarily indicated by the two terms (perhaps not very felicitous, if only because they necessarily imply a hierarchy) of "structure" and "superstructure," with a relationship of "determination or "causation" in the proper sense. Through this confusion, "superstructure" would become mechanically caused by the "structure." That is, given a particular structure one would necessarily have a particular superstructure and no other.

Once the relationship of structure and superstructure has been interpreted in this manner, it is clear that one cannot logically escape the most antiquated causalistic mechanicism. Any concept of the "relative autonomy" of the superstructural sphere, including the very voluntaristic impulse which guides decisions of the political structure and development of class consciousness, especially as implied in the passage from the class in itself (*an sich*) to the class for itself (*für sich*) collapses. It is true, on the other hand, that—still citing the same extract—Marx strongly stresses, referring to the figurative form of the aphorism, how *Sein macht das Denken* (literally, "being makes thinking," not vice versa). Hence one cannot blame all the misunderstanding on the crudeness or the lack of *esprit de finesse* of the commentators.

In their favor, one can raise well-founded attenuating circumstances. It has in fact been remarked that "this relationship (between structure and superstructure) should not be understood, as has too often been the case, among followers as well as opponents of Marx, as a relationship of mechanical determination on the part of an 'economic factor' artificially isolated from the totality of social relations. In fact, the relationship is dialectical and expresses itself in the context of a complex dialect between structural and superstructural elements. It is a dialectic which recognizes not only the *action* of the structure on the superstructure, but also the *reaction* of the superstructure on the structure, just as reciprocal interaction exists between the different spheres and elements of the superstructure. In reality, 'structure' and 'superstructure' are only linguistic metaphors which are intended to emphasize the basic importance in the totality of social relations, of relations of production—without, however, proposing mechanical one-way determinations."[7]

I wanted to quote this passage at length because it seemed to me indicative of an attitude quite widespread among contemporary Marxists. In the first place, it is an attempt to reevaluate the superstructural element so thoroughly as thus to make it possible to establish a perfectly logical continuity—not only historical, but also through its internal coherence—

between Marxism and Leninism, seeing in Lenin someone who voluntaristically foresees in superstructural terms a revolutionary politics for which the "structure" was clearly not yet mature. Second, the aim is to bring out the interpretative and logical consequences to which this restoration necessarily leads: that is, the devaluation of the differentiation between the structure and the superstructure which for this purpose are presented as simple "linguistic metaphors." The least one can say is that here we are confronted with an excess of zeal. This means, therefore, on its part a series of somewhat out-of-focus formulations in which all phenomena seem nebulously to lie on the same plane, involved, so it would seem, in a vague process of interaction between "different spheres" and "different elements."

Engels's explanation is more convincing. He recognizes that the Marxist formulation is rather hasty, and is not without some pressure, since it was concerned with polemically asserting a materialist point of view against the prevalent idealistic point of view of the dominant bourgeois ideology. In the famous letter to Joseph Bloch, Engels asserts that we should not omit the "reciprocal action" of the superstructure on the structure (*umwälzende Praxis*): "According to the materialist conception of history, the *ultimately* determining element in history is the production and reproduction of real life. More than this neither Marx nor I have ever asserted. Hence if somebody twists this into saying that the economic element is the *only* determining one, he transforms that proposition into a meaningless, abstract, senseless phrase. The economic situation is the basis, but the various elements of the superstructure—political forms of the class struggle and its results, to wit: constitutions established by the victorious class after a successful battle, etc., juridical forms, and even the reflexes of all these actual struggles in the brains of the participants; political, juristic, philosophical theories, religious views and their further development into systems of dogmas—also exercise their influence upon the course of the historical struggles and in many cases preponderate in determining their *form*. There is an interaction of all these elements, in which, amid all the endless host of accidents (that is, of things and events whose inner interconnection is so remote or so impossible of proof that we can regard it as nonexistent, as negligible), the economic movement finally asserts itself as necessary. Otherwise the application of the theory to any period of history would be easier than the solution of a simple equation of the first degree."[8]

THE SPECIFICATION OF THE DIALECTICAL RELATION BETWEEN STRUCTURE AND SUPERSTRUCTURE

Engels's text is perceptive but the elaborations—given also the occasional nature of the exchange of letters—are very far from being exhaustive or conceptually rigorous. He seems to be able to distinguish, within the "superstructure," a first level or sphere, the "politico-juridical," and then a second level with a higher degree of abstraction and distancing from the economic base, of a conceptual kind in the truly philosophical sense.

However, all the questions related to the "correspondence" hypothesized between the economic base and the superstructural sphere remain vague. To speak of "interaction" means remaining within an approximate sociologizing formula. To invoke the "dialectic" may seem more rigorous, but then it is necessary to go forward to the specification of this dialectical connection which, once it has been confirmed, poses the delicate problem of establishing the method of proof of indeterminate historical situations.

In fact, so as to pose correctly the problem of relationship between structure and structural formations, one must go back to Marxist thought as a whole and question its whole apparatus. In particular, the following concepts are basic:

a) Division of labor, as already laid out in the classical economists whom Marx was to criticize, particularly as they dehistoricized specific historical situations by eternalizing them. However, from them he was to take all the analytic instruments which could be useful for his critical analysis of capitalism as a global system.

b) The situation of the productive forces, or level of technical development in the sense of industrial machinery (or "system of machines"), but also social—as social organization of collective labor.

c) Mode of production (*Produktionsweisser*), that is, the way in which men procure the means of subsistence, hence the form in which the mode of production is developing; hence, bearing in mind how—according to Hegel's famous formula—"the being of men coincides with their production," the mode in which and with which human beings live in society, producing their means of subsistence and thus, by reproducing these means, reproducing themselves.

d) Relations of production tied to the mode of production in that the mode of production implies the man-nature relation (or man who exploits nature), but at the same time also implies the man-man relation in the sense of the relation between man who exploits nature by exploiting the labor of another man as a tool or instrument to exploit nature. Hence relations of production are established by interpersonal relations crystallized into specific social roles and made necessary by a particular level achieved in a given era by the forces of production. To the latter, human beings are bound independently of their tastes or their personal preferences but rather as living in society within the social organization.

A PROBLEM TO EXPLORE: NATURE AS
FOUNDATION OF THE CONCEPT OF STRUCTURE

According to Marx, the historical form achieved by the process of production as a whole in a given era gives rise to a specific economic-social formation, marked by a specific type of division of labor, a particular position of the productive forces, a determinate mode of production and specific relations of production within specific forms of property and a specific legitimating ideology.

Applying to Marx himself a basic canon of historical materialism, the *historical nature* of the *economic categories* was correctly brought out. On the basis of this nature, the development of the categories depends also on real historical development. Marx's structural theory, that is, his basic concept of "structure," is able to provide "an abstractly general . . . suprahistorical schema of reference, and at the same time to give it a specific content in a determinate 'model' whose specific laws of functioning will depend on the particular historical conditions of each epoch and will be valid only for and under these conditions."[9]

What until recently, however, commentators have neglected, has been the foundation of the position of the forces of production, that is, the *natural elements in the real sense*, from the biogenetic enjoyment of individuals to the data concerning the geographical, geological, vegetable, and animal environment. These elements, concretely present at times in a dramatic fashion in current discussions of ecology, have not attracted all the attention required either from Marxists or from Marx himself.

Only in Engels does one see a greater sensitivity regarding this particular aspect of the makeup of society, but his sensitivity does not always free itself from a crude, reifying positivistic approach. The concept of "productive forces" certainly also includes natural forces, from basic raw materials to various types of energy. But this concerns natural forces taken for granted and a priori believed to be inexhaustible, in a perspective which, at least in this aspect, links Marx to the somewhat generic progressivism of his age—as one can, moreover, see in the eulogy woven into the *Manifesto* to the bourgeoisie for its function of drastic modernization.

Essentially, the vision that Marx and Engels have of society is strictly dichotomous. This conception does not see in society a totality of scattered individuals, distributed and gathered together by chance, nor yet a conglomerate of highly mobile organized groups (the neopluralist, utilitarian-hedonistic hypothesis). Marx and Engels see society as a dynamic process, dominated by a tendential bipolarity, that is, as a terrain of differentiation and conflict between social classes (bourgeoisie and proletariat) conceived of as decisive historical subjects.

The last point is reasserted in relation to the attempt to empty Marxism by depriving it of any substantial content, so as to reduce it to a mere canon of historiographic enquiry. The first years of this century, in the wake of the powerful antiscientific and neoidealistic reaction, which then made itself felt with extraordinary simultaneity in Henri Bergson in France, the neo-Hegelians in Italy, the insistence on psychologizing factors in Germany, as the "spirit of capitalism" in Max Weber and Werner Sombart, and especially in Croce's *Materialismo storico ed economia Marxistica*, gave rise to an operation of theoretical systematization with important political off-shoots. Antonio Gramsci noted this. It tended essentially to redefine Marxism to the point of making it a kind of "methodological preface" for the use of historians so that they did not neglect in their research the economic and social conditions of the situations and historical periods being analyzed. More recently, the "nouveau philosophes" in France, romantically drawn to soothe the disappointments after May 1968, with convenient doses of individualistic spontaneism to the point of para-literary irrationalism, repeated the same attempt to empty Marxism; so, too, the Liberal-Democrats in Italy who tend to present representative parliamentary democracy as a historical *ne plus ultra*. They are aided by instinctive Marxists who prefer to sanctify Marxism and recite axioms as though they were exclamations, instead of trying to do today what Marx and Engels did for their time.

As I have observed elsewhere, in this perspective it is very important to grasp and confirm the definitions of man and essential human activity— or human action provided with meaning in a determinate historical horizon—which are related to Marxism seen as an open global system. For Marx, in the *Economic and Philosophical Manuscripts of 1844*, "Man is directly a natural being. As a natural being and as a living natural being, he is on the one hand endowed with natural powers, vital powers—he is an *active* natural being. These forces exist in him as tendencies and abilities— as *instincts*. On the other hand, as a natural, corporeal, sensuous, objective being, he is a *suffering*, conditioned and limited creature, like animals and plants."[10]

It would seem, in a hurried and insufficiently critical reading, that here Marx cites as Herbert Spencer might have done, and it was not by chance that many Marxists at the end of the century, especially in Italian culture, and despite Antonio Labriola's polemical clarifications, thought they could identify the new "trinity" in Marx, Darwin, and Spencer. What, however, might appear as an essentially mechanistic and passive evolutionism, unilinearly cumulative and without drama, is at once made clear in Marx as an activity which is not purely naturalistic. Man is a natural being, but he is also something radically different: "But man is not merely a natural being: he is a *human* natural being. That is to say, he is a being for himself. . . . Therefore, *human* objects are not natural objects as they immediately present themselves, and neither is *human sense*, as it immediately is—as it is objectively—*human* sensibility, human objectivity."[11]

In other words, man is nature but is not only nature. Indeed, man does not have a nature in the same way as the plant, the mineral, or the rock. Man does not have a nature but a history. He is born, develops, and becomes in history, and not necessarily in *historical*, rationalizing history, diachronically directed toward an inevitable betterment, but in an open dramatic history in which all eventualities are possible and there is nothing taken for granted, a "human, too human" history, without otherworldly supports and designs of providence. In fact, "And as everything natural has to *come into being*, man too has his act of origin—*history*—which, however, is for him a known history, and hence as an act of origin it is a conscious, self-transcending act of origin. History is the true natural history of man."[12] The concept of "consciousness" is not, however, hypostasized in Marx, as happens instead in all idealistic philosophies. Consciousness in Marx does not remain, nor is it reduced to an act of pure self-contemplation: it is transformed into a project, it becomes action with a view to the end and necessarily refers to conscious action. Man's consciousness is activity, work, vital expression, and production. This characteristically Marxist connection of the essence of man to his labor directed to the satisfaction of determinate needs is for Marx the guarantee against traditional metaphysics falling back into a gratuitous relativism, without prospects and which would preclude any reasoned evaluation of specific determinate situations. "Human essence" is not given once and for all, as dogmatic theologies and philosophies would like. It is valid as a concept-limit (*Grenz-Begriff*) against which to evaluate specific situations in their practical material manifestation, but a task to achieve at the level of historical experience, by confronting the evolutionary capacity, that is, the historicity of its needs. Man is a measure for man. In this sense, Marx believes in history but is not a historicist. His point of departure is practice but he does not drown in it. "Man," he wrote in the *Manuscripts*, "makes of his vital activity itself the object of his will and consciousness. He has a conscious vital activity: *there is not a determinate sphere with which he immediately confuses himself.*"[13] Yet again, in the eighth thesis on Feuerbach, "All social life is essentially practical. All mysteries which lead theory to mysticism find their rational solution in human practice and in the comprehension of this practice."[14] Marx is therefore not a historicist and, on the other hand, he cannot be considered a structuralist in the sense of one who formulates propositions supposed to be synchronically valid beyond any "historical horizon." It is not by chance that Marx speaks of socialism as the end of the "prehistory of humanity" and the beginning of human history in the real sense, that

is, of a non-alienated history, but rather "restored" to man, or recon-
quered by him.

NOTES

1. See, in this regard, G. Poggi in his introduction to the anthology *Karl Marx*,
Bologna: Il Mulino, 1977, pp. 7ff.
2. Despite the brilliant nature of his prose, this is what happens in the first
chapters of Joseph Schumpeter's *Capitalism, Socialism and Democracy*, New York:
Harper and Brothers, 1942.
3. See G. Therborn, *La classe operaia e la nascita del marxismo*, in *Comunità*, n. 178,
August 1977, p. 144.
4. The formula "critical realism" was used by G. D. H. Cole in his *What
Marx Really Meant*, London, 1934; new ed.: *The Meaning of Marxism*, London: V.
Gollanez, 1948. However, a similar formula is to be found in the work Veblen
dedicated to "some neglected points in the theory of socialism." It should however be noticed that in Anglo-Saxon culture, the reference to realism, however
critical, is always done pragmatically, essentially in an a-dialectical sense or at
least de-dialectic, which clearly means a grave misunderstanding of the whole
Marxist construct.
5. See Marx's preface to *A Contribution to the Critique of Political Economy*, in
K. Marx & F. Engels, *Selected Works*, New York: International Publishers, 1968,
p. 182.
6. Marx's preface, pp. 182–83.
7. U. Melotti, *Marx*, Firenze: Vallecchi, 1974, pp. 58–59.
8. F. Engels, "Letter to J. Bloch in Königsberg, 21 September 1890," in Marx &
Engels, *Selected Works*, p. 692.
9. G. Carandini, *La struttura economica della società nelle opere di Marx*, Padova:
Marsilio, 1973, pp. 90–91.
10. K. Marx, *Economic and Philosophical Manuscripts of 1844*, Collected Works, vol.
3, New York: International Publishers, 1965, p. 336.
11. Marx, *Economic and Philosophical Manuscripts*, p. 337.
12. Marx, *Economic and Philosophical Manuscripts*, p. 337.
13. K. Marx, *Manoscritti economico-filosofici del 1844*, trans. by N. Bobbio, Torino:
Einaudi, 1968, p. 78 (my emphasis).
14. Marx, *Selected Works*, vol. 5, p. 5.

4

✢

Pierre-Joseph Proudhon: Justice as the Basis of Human Coexistence

THE PRIDE OF THE PROVINCIAL

Marx's negative judgment and sarcasm have long weighed on Proudhon. To Marx, Proudhon's reputation was due to a strange misunderstanding which made him pass for a great philosopher or economist whether for the educated German or French public. However, more than once when Marx was short of decisive logical arguments he covered himself by means of a witty remark or a sharply polemical attack. To give a revealing example, think of the problem of the origin of property. Marx states that the bourgeoisie is basically marked by possession of property, but does not then clarify how property, or "primitive accumulation," is historically formed. When up against it, he is ironical about, and derides, the disenchanted traditional virtues of love of work and savings. But, as Schumpeter also noted, to be sarcastic does not mean to explain.

However, some of the responsibility for the grossest misunderstandings, which made him by turns pass as a renegade of the proletariat, a reactionary who sold out the bourgeoisie, or the promoter of a generic anarchic rebelliousness, must be placed on Proudhon himself: that is, to his method of presenting his ideas, to the style which often sacrifices precision to impulsiveness, and the timid aggressiveness of the provincial which stayed with him all his life. Having completed his studies with all the difficulties typical of anyone in chronically straitened economic circumstances, Proudhon began to travel from one end of France to the other to escape his limited native horizons and at the same time to assert his own autonomy. He was ready, as he wrote at age twenty-eight in the curriculum vitae sent in 1837 to the Academy at Besançon, "to tell the truth face to face to an employer," and to be victim of his "provincial pride." In fact, one may say that Proudhon always bore with him the "provinces," though trying desperately to escape from them. To the end, he remained a man of the periphery, outside the main game, a classic provincial: isolated, intolerant, and moralistic, he was pushed to radicalize his positions, on the basis of real timidity, but precisely for this reason a natural opponent of centralized organization, bureaucratic unanimity, and pseudo-general interests.

One can understand the alarm of his contemporaries which Saint-Beuve recalled with masterly assurance: Proudhon was not a plausible observer: he had too much bile, and this colored his objects. He had in his head a whole future society, which made current society intolerable and hateful to him. He was not sufficiently empirical nor adequately disinterested to take the pulse of things coolly and precisely point to the crises. One can also understand Proudhon's own discomfort under the systematic accusation of utopianism when his predictions were coming true before everyone's eyes, while his ideas remained uncredited.

On the significance of many of Proudhon's themes in the latter part of the twentieth century there is now no doubt. The Marx–Proudhon polemic, contrary to its appearances, is basically ending up in Proudhon's favor. The day after the tragic events in Hungary and the Polish crisis, when one was dealing with events which were still hot, I noted that their historical importance, what made them something vastly more important than a town riot, lay essentially in the direction they indicated: a return to the "base": a rediscovery of the original and unsurpassable functions, from the point of view of basic democracy and socialism, of the small group and spontaneous associations as they appear and act at the level of the local community and at the factory level: the reevaluation of real, short-term interests tied to individuals. I ended by stating that this was not only the echo of Gramsci's teaching: it was really the return of Proudhon.

THE RETURN TO COUNTERPOWERS OF THE BASE

One may say that every day this return gets new, unexpected confirmation. In Europe the socialist tradition is freeing itself from maximalist dreams, and is becoming aware of the "cunning of the concept" implicit in the acritical, miracle-believing adoption of the dialectical schema, which tends to confuse predicted things with real ones. This can result in a very high-priced political mistake. The belief that social reforms are not accomplished just by ordering them, but by doing them, is also gaining ground. There is a problem of means and instruments. Planning is not a touchstone, and furthermore there are different plans. There is an omni-competent, totalitarian plan, the necessary expression of the centripetal, monolithic State, and there is flexible, democratic planning based on the "judgment of the community," as the Americans phrase it most felici-tously. In other words, there is a problem of "correct technique" in re-forms which has to be resolved at the outset if one wants to induce an ef-fective "organic reformism," inflexible as idea but at the same time technically aware. Furthermore, the critique of political parties and par-liamentary democracy is no longer the monopoly of the right. In this re-gard the observations produced on the left are important and are giving rise to important convergences, from Jayaprakash Narayan to Ignazio Silone and Adriano Olivetti. They are no longer outdated, more or less in-tolerant protests, but now offer elements and starting points for a system-atic body of doctrine. They tackle head on the question of power: its for-mation, legitimacy, and management; they put the problem of the democratic State, structurally based on action from beneath and on pop-ular participation, in a new light.

These are the themes of Proudhon's reflections, his original contribu-tion to the socialist tradition and the meaning and purpose of his work. Contrary to the generally authoritarian and centralized approach of the Marxists, Proudhon showed consistently the value of the need for diffu-sion of power at all levels of collective life and of a socialism based on the interconnected, dynamic federation of the producers instead of on the omnipotence of a centripetal, oppressive State. A mere summary descrip-tion of Proudhon's thought is enough to document the central position which such a conception of a solid, but pluralistic society, balanced but dynamic, occupied.

JUSTICE AS IDEA AND STRENGTH

The mainspring of all progress according to Proudhon is justice. However, the idea of justice, if it is to be effective, cannot be restricted to the inter-nal awareness of the individual or to abstract certainty. It must be trans-formed into a force of ideas, able to influence directly the structure and or-ganization of society. Faced with this task, positive religions are powerless. In fact, their common basis is transcendance. They thus op-press and condition from without, with the fear of punishment or the promise of rewards, the spirit of the individual. Thus, for example, "Christianity, through its beginning, all its theology, is the condemnation of the human ego, contempt for the person, rape of conscience. . . .The nat-ural state of man is one of sin: how thus could the Christian respect the person of his brother? . . . To raise up this fallen being and restore him, there is precisely required the sacrifice of a heavenly victim, repeated daily in hundreds of thousands of places simultaneously. . . . In this way Christianity, having to triumph over the exaggeration of the ego, had to exaggerate its humiliation. Its mission was thus not to establish justice but to prepare the ground in which it could germinate. *Justumque terra germinet.* Not only does it exclude this from humanity by its theology, it makes it impossible by the elimination of personal dignity, with all its institutions and symbols."[1]

Proudhon brings out these very same contradictions in the attitude of Christianity as regards equality: "In Christianity, the condition of persons is not the same. As we shall see, inequality comes by providence. It is necessary that one part—the most numerous of humanity—should *serve* the other. In order to obtain this service one must sacrifice human dignity."[2] For Proudhon, Christian society offers no other show than that of a "refined feudalism," wherein justice has no effective social force and the State itself, which ought to present itself as guarantor of the common good, really "finds itself obliged to defend the unjust." He elaborates: "The aim of the State lies in organizing, doing and enforcing justice. Justice is the essential attribute, the principal function of the State. . . . Justice, the law of the moral world, material and intellectual world, has its basic rule in equality. However, in the two periods of civilization, paganism and Christianity, equality suffered from a drastic reduction because of the generally accepted fact of the inequality of wealth. From this it occurred that the State, set up by justice, is found to be at the same time for the defense of something which in itself is not just and which exists only by means of ignorance and self-interest, in such a way that the action of the State becomes contradictory."[3]

Proudhon believes that in order to justify inequality of wealth two theories are mainly invoked—the pagan one of Fate and the Christian one of Providence, which are basically equal, in that "there is this in common between the two theories, that the church of Christ and that of Fate both have their *raisons d'état.*" The dominant principle is thus not justice but rather authority. "Justice is subordinated to *raison d'état*: the state is not the result of a contract which emanates from the citizens and gives obligations from one to another, but rather it is the result of the relation of subordination expressed by these two terms—Authority which commands no longer in the name of necessity but in the name of salvation, and the subject who obeys."[4]

Already from the extracts quoted, the basis of the anarchic egalitarianism which marks Proudhon's thought is clear. "All the individuals of which society is made up are, in principle, of the same being, the same calibre, type, and model: if we see differences between them, these arise not from the creating thought which has produced their being and form, but from the external circumstances of the environment in which individual characteristics are born and developed. It is not through this inequality—furthermore exceptionally exaggerated—that society survives, even against its will."[5] Proudhon's egalitarian passion leads him to minimize all the differences to be met with in daily experience. He recognizes no real diversity of talent, intelligence, and so forth, but rather a diversity of attitudes, developed in various ways. As regards the inequality of the races, Proudhon somewhat qualifies his own egalitarianism, and saves himself from the contradiction by observing that "catholicism makes a great noise regarding the unitary origin of our species." And he continues by asserting that when equality is not found in nature, men think about finding it. Proudhon believed that the role of true political economy lay precisely in creating equality, wherein there lay only the chance variation of economic phenomena and the fluctuations of the market. He argued, in fact, that science must dominate phenomena, not submit to them. It must mediate between the minimums and maximums between which the curve of frequency of phenomena develops. For Proudhon, equality in all areas of life and social activity is the realization of the universal principle of justice, which is the only real guarantee of progress. He believes the moral equality of persons (the basis of true reciprocal respect) and equality of functions (the key point of political economy) to be indispensable, and ultimately equality of wealth and incomes. This will not result in the general leveling and mediocratizing of values: on the contrary, a hierarchy will remain based on real merits and services rendered, instead of on a caste or class superiority, or privileges which destroy equality.

EQUALITY AND THE FEDERAL PRINCIPLE

Equality is the practical correlative of justice in the social field and that of ethical relations. The notion of balance, together with that of equality, which is its basic premise, is the key to Proudhonian sociology. Without equality there is no balance: to be really "balanced," true power must above all be on an equal footing. Without parity, there is only the dominance of one force over another and the consequent formation of a centralized, oppressive bloc. Balance thus requires the federative principle. Indeed, in the sphere of ethics balance involves mutual respect for persons; in the field of economics a balanced harmony between agricultural and industrial groups (mutualism of producers); and in the field of politics collaboration coordinated between states and nations (federalism). Balance is thus not only the realization of the principle of justice, based on the idea of equality. It is also the condition for order and progress.

The need expressed by Proudhon in the theory of equilibrium was to be taken up, in different tones and with no concession to the myth of progress and humanitarianism, by Vilfredo Pareto, with his formula of social balance, which means a radical distrust of any reformist scheme. Proudhon, instead, foresees the objection: if the two pans of the scale are in perfect equilibrium, there is no more movement, life stops, there is universal paralysis. He replies: "possibly equilibrium corresponds to paralysis and to zero in the world of the Absolute, but we know nothing of this. The fact is that in real life everything is movement and development: fixed and eternal are only the laws of movement itself."[6] Man's task is consciously to help this movement and to develop himself in orderly fashion, in harmony with the supreme principle of justice: "We are drawn on with the universe in a constant metamorphosis, which is realized the more surely and gloriously as we ourselves develop intelligence and morality."[7]

Equilibrium and its corollaries (philosophical, economical, and political) make up the substratum of the basic ideas of Proudhon's sociology. In this, society does not appear as a monolithic structure, but as a complex of groups differing in their orientation and interests, though variously interdependent. Proudhon believed in the existence of a "collective being" which essentially corresponds to the "natural sociality" of man. Each, he noted, is simultaneously person and collectivity, individual and family, citizen and people, human being and humanity. It is on the basis of "collective spirit," that Proudhon enters by right into the history of sociological thought. However, it should be clearly brought out that Proudhon's collective being should not replace, as an abstract formula, the observation of concrete human groups. Proudhon's society is not simply the incarnation of the "collective being." If it were not balanced by the observation of concrete, differentiated human groups, this idea would be no more than a *fictio mentis*. Far from being contradictory, Proudhon's thought shows here a typical complexity, or the attempt to reconcile in ultimate equilibrium individualistic and social needs. These two realities—society and individual—though different and at times contradictory cannot be separated without making them unintelligible. In the *Philosophie du progrès*, he defines society as a *sui generis being* composed of the fluid relationship (*rapport fluide*) and the economic solidarity of all individuals. In the *Pornocratie* he added, so as to avoid possible misunderstandings in an atomistic sense: "Collectivities, groups, genders, species are not pure fictions of our intellect: they are realities as real as the individualities, monads, and molecules which constitute them, under the same heading as these last."[8]

THE INTEGRATION OF THE INDIVIDUAL IN THE GROUP

It is this special integration of individual and group which forms the basis for the development of collective strength, which is not the simple result of the sum of individual efforts, but rather contains a synthetic power, consequently one properly of the group, superior as regards quality and energy to the sum of the elementary forces which constitute it. This is true also for the State, or the "joining together of several groups different by nature and aim, each formed for exercising a particular function and the creation of a particular product—thus, joined together under a common law and in an identical interest."[9] The false problem which, particularly in Comte and Spencer, tended abstractly to counterpose individual and society, seems to be grasped in its real terms by Proudhon, who makes the theory of collective reason follow on from that of collective force: the former's task lies precisely in balancing and counterbalancing individual egoisms, confronting them systematically with the needs of social life.

The necessity of such an integration for the stability and at the same time the development of civil society is called upon, and emerges, in all Proudhon's works. It is the nub of his pluralistic conceptions. He distrusted the controls of authority and rejected excessive standardizations, even if they were dictated by a supposed rationality. In the *System of Economic Contradictions: or, The Philosophy of Misery*, Proudhon wrote that there were things to be done by other than the great social or national unit, in fact, many more things which should be done by collective units of a lower order: of the department, of the commune, of industrial and commercial units, the numerous family units, and above all the innumerable individual units. The same demand was expressed by Proudhon in *De la capacité politique des classes ouvrières*. He writes of a special pluralistic conception of social renewal, wherein reformist intervention cannot "explode" from a single center of political management, but must rather arise spontaneously in the various productive sectors and the initiative of the base: that is, from concrete workers' groups. It is this spontaneous origin, productively motivated, and from beneath, which guarantees the organic, or complete, character of the social revolution, both vertically and horizontally. Indeed, a social revolution is a new organism replacing a decrepit organization. This substitution is not done in an instant. A truly organic revolution is a product of universal life, not of any single individual.

In this light, Proudhon makes a basic criticism of communist doctrine, above all in its Marxist version, and counterposes his own theory, which has as its premises operative plurality, autonomous, differentiated initiative from below, and the predominance of the economic over the political sphere. According to him, the political system created by communist doctrine can be defined as a compact democracy, apparently based on the dictatorship of the masses. However, these masses, in reality, are ensured universal slavery under a centralized authority invested with undivided power. It exercises the systematic destruction of every individual thought, corporative or local, which may be thought deviant. Universal suffrage is organized so as to support this anonymous tyranny through the maintenance of a mediocre majority, always against able citizens and independent characters, who are labeled as suspect and always few in number.

It is certainly possible to have reservations about Proudhon's political and sociological system. At the beginning of the chapter, I pointed out the criticisms set forth by Marx, especially in the essay "The Poverty of Philosophy," written in response to Proudhon's *System of Economic Contradictions: or, The Philosophy of Misery*. Georges Sorel expressed other reservations, especially as regards the fact that Proudhon had neglected to study the experience of the old rural democracies.[10] However, the extraordinary insights, like the one descibed above, in which Proudhon's work is rich, justify the overall judgment of Sorel, a judgment whose immediate relevance it is hardly necessary to stress: "For too long, socialism has pursued a bad path, under the inspiration of *bad shepherds*, whose formation was carried out by democracy. There is nothing more essential for the future of the proletariat than to begin with Proudhon's teachings. The disciples (or supposed disciples) of Marx, by waging relentless campaigns against Proudhon, bear a large part of the responsibility for the decadence of socialism. What is cosmic is that these second-rate intellectuals have denounced as *bourgeois* this admirable representative of the world of labor, whom Daniel Halévy was right to define as: a perfect type of the peasant, the French artisan, a hero of our people."[11]

NOTES

1. P. J. Proudhon, *De la justice dans la Révolution et dans l'Église*, Paris: Lacroix, 1858, pp. 57–58.

2. Proudhon, *De la justice dans la Révolution et dans l'Église*, p. 67.

3. Proudhon, *De la justice dans la Révolution et dans l'Église*, p. 69.

4. Proudhon, *De la justice dans la Révolution et dans l'Église*, p. 75.

5. Proudhon, *De la justice dans la Révolution et dans l'Église*, p. 69.

6. Proudhon, *Philosophie du progrès*, Bruxelles: Labèque, 1859, p. 49.

7. Proudhon, *De la justice dans la Révolution et dans l'Église*, p. 232.

8. Proudhon, *La pornocratie, ou les femmes dans les temps modernes*, Paris: Lacroix, 1875, p. 395.

9. Proudhon, *La pornocratie, ou les femmes dans les temps modernes*, p. 481.

10. G. Sorel, *Materiaux d'une théorie du prolétariat*, Paris: Rivière, 1919, p. 393.

11. Sorel, *Materiaux d'une théorie du prolétariat*, p. 394.

5

+

Émile Durkheim: The Problem of Lost Solidarity

AGAINST HEDONISTIC AND UTILITARIAN INDIVIDUALISM

As for Saint-Simon and Comte, for Durkheim too the basic problem posed to sociology is that of the reconstruction of the social order. In other words, it is the problem of lost solidarity, which must be rediscovered and founded scientifically. Thus, foremost in Durkheim there is a moral choice, which is also a choice of value and at the same time a philosophical premise. For Durkheim, sociology is not a mere technique, something which can be reduced to "social engineering." However, it is also true that in Durkheim sociology is clearly distanced from philosophy, even if philosophical discussion is not forgotten. He criticized fundamentally the *généralité* of his predecessors, especially that of Spencer and Comte. He found their sociology was still too little scientific, positivist only in the programmatic sense—in words only, that is—and in fact still philosophizing, abstract, and generic. Durkheim meant to make sociology a science in the specific sense, provided with its own object and methodological rules: that is, the science of social facts. As for Saint-Simon and Comte there was the painful, dramatic precedent of the 1789 Revolution, so too for Durkheim the French society in which he, an Alsatian and a Jew, was born and raised, appeared shaken by deep crises. First was the 1871 Commune, just after the disastrous defeat at the hands of Prussia at Sedan in 1870, the first stage and premise for a tragic game of reprisals which was to unreel between the Treaty of Versailles, the fall of Paris in 1940, and that of Berlin in 1945. Second, the Dreyfus case was to reveal the xenophobic, anti-Semitic, and crudely chauvinistic spirit of certain sectors of

the bourgeoisie; last, the serious, prolonged tensions regarding the relations between state and church, especially as related to the lay, "public"
character of education, and the school system in general.

These tensions in French society are continually present and active in
Durkheim's thought, and explain some basic characteristics: his essential
conservatism; his severely critical attitude toward hedonistic, utilitarian
individualism; the attempt to transcend both the anarchistic revolution-
ism of the Commune and, at the same time, the nostalgic attractions of the
restoration of the monarchy; and thus, the commitment to build a lay
morality, republican, able to provide not only a coldly juridical, but also
an emotionally rich base for the Third Republic, threatened from without
by the combined pressures of revolutionaries and monarchists, and from
within by an unprecedented wave of corruption. It is no wonder that
Durkheim's sociology is thus marked by contradictory aspects. He criticizes classical political economy because it made the individual the starting and finishing point of every economic, political, and social action. But
at the same time, he never tired of insisting that the theoretical opposition
between individual and society is a useless problem, as there is no individual without society, in the very clear sense that the individual could
not even survive outside the social framework, while it is not possible
even to think of society without referring to individuals. He could never
forgive Spencer for making social equilibrium depend on the game of mutual blackmail and individual egoisms, but there is no doubt that, at least
in this respect, Spencer's construct has a coherence lacking in Durkheim's.
As regards Saint-Simon, while he accepted his basic principle that economic life must be subject to an organized, collective action, and thus
must move forward to a socialistic coordination by social groups and their
activities, he then stressed Saint-Simon's error which, in his view, was total as regards what is currently the cause of social malaise, and thus ended
up by proposing "an aggravation of the evil as a cure."[1]

In Durkheim's criticisms of Saint-Simon, there emerges a feature he had
in common with Freud: a certain pessimism, concerning the natural tendency of the individual to recognize the good and follow its rules, to control himself, to avoid excesses and rages on the basis of the sense of pro-
portion of classical wisdom (*ne quid nimis*). In this sense, the
revolutionaries seemed to him ingenuously optimistic or simply superficial. As regards Saint-Simon, for example, and his "industrial solution,"
Durkheim remarked that "though in principle his philanthropic morality
was basically purely industrial, he realized that in order to ensure order,
it was necessary to enable it to dominate the sphere of industrial interests,
by thereby attributing to it a religious character. In this passage there is
something which does not perfectly agree with the industrialist principle
and indeed is possibly its best refutation. . . . It is not the sentiment of cos-

mic feeling, even if expressed in a tangible form which can dominate egoisms and effectively make men agree. Where, then, are those moral forces
capable of setting up, having accepted, and maintaining, the necessary
discipline?" In this last question, there is all the anxiety and at the same
time the deep motivatedness of the purpose of Durkheim's sociology. He
continued: "This is not the place to deal with the problem"—revealing his
conservative approach, however enlightened—"however, one may observe that among the institutions of the former regime, there is one Saint-
Simon does not mention, and yet which, transformed, would be open to
harmonize with our current state of affairs. This concerns professional
groupings or corporations."[2]

THE OVERTURNING OF THE MARXIST PERSPECTIVE

Possibly this passage suffices to let us intuit the distance between
Durkheim and Marx. However, this undoubted distance was not due in
Durkheim to crude misunderstandings, however common to the period.
One cannot find in the passages Durkheim devotes to Marxist historical
materialism, especially when reviewing A. Labriola's work, any of the
usual misunderstandings which tended to equate Marx to Spencer or
make him the mere counterpart of Charles Darwin for the social sciences.[3]
It has been rightly observed that "Durkheim's interpretation of Marxism
. . . is lucid and precise . . . an example as regards the naturalistic interpretations of certain Marxists à la Kautsky which date from the same time.
It is enough to remember that Durkheim recognizes in historical materialism not a dependence of social phenomena from hunger, thirst, the desire for procreation, etc., but from the state achieved by human activity."[4]
However, on the whole, Durkheim's assessment of Marxism is heavily
negative. He accepts the idea whereby social life is to be explained not by
the judgment which people connected to it make of it, but rather by the
underlying causes which escape individual consciousness. However,
Durkheim does not see these causes as at all determinate or at least linked
to the economic structure, as the Marxists do. Rather, these causes seem to
him tied to the "collective consciousness," while in his view they are
wholly independent of the socialist movement. To Durkheim, this conclusion may easily be reached before Marx, and without him. In fact, we are
dealing with a conception which represents "the logical outlet for all the
historical and psychological movement of these last fifty years. For a long
time, historians have realized that social evolution has causes which are
not recognized by the agents of historical events. . . . At the same time, individual psychology has taught us that the consciousness of the individual often reflects the underlying state of the organism. . . . Socialism has

been able to use this idea for its own advantage, but it did not produce it and above all it is not implicit in it." And further on, "Not only is the Marxist hypothesis not proved, but it conflicts with facts which seem firmly irrefutable. Sociologists and historians seem increasing to agree in the common definition that religion is the first of all social phenomena. . . . In principle, everything is religious."[5]

The Marxist perspective is clearly overturned. Much more radically than for Weber, who tended to accept Marxism as a working hypothesis (that is, when cleansed of any dogmatic one-sidedness), for Durkheim at the base of society there is not economic activity but rather religious participation. This is scarcely the moment to warn that Durkheim's reconstruction of Marxism is deeply polemical, and that he tends not to see in it what Marx valued most: the dialectical connection whereby it is not permissible to counterpose economic structure and political, ideological, religious, juridical—and so on—superstructure. However, it is true that while Durkheim attempts a synthesis between sociology and anthropology which was to take him, from *Rules of Sociological Method* to *Elementary Forms of Religious Life*, there is in his thought neither room nor a consideration for acknowledgment of the notions of historico-social change and economic development. He is logically sociocentric and, in this sense, he is the legitimate successor of Comte.

This does not mean that for Durkheim society is only a datum. It is also a historical duty, a reality to be constructed, an aim. Durkheim's insistence on the basic conditions which make possible, and hence relatively secure, the social order, are connected not with negation, but rather the deep awareness of the crisis of industrial societies. His concept of "anomie" is parallel to that of "alienation" and is presented as the expression of the state of relative uprootedness in which human groups have come to find themselves as a result of a process of too rapid and too technistically produced industrialization in the following points: workers in the mass organized according to military logic and concentrated into often unhealthy factories; the isolation of the workers who are mostly forced by day to live apart from their family and in general from their natural community; specialized workers, more technically informed than peasants formerly, but also forced infinitely to repeat the same movements, hence reduced to machines or, more correctly, to appendages of machines.

THE DEFENSE AND REEVALUATION
OF THE DIVISION OF LABOR

Despite everything, the division of labor, which for Marx as for the other socialists should be abolished through the abolition of private property in the means of production, should according to Durkheim rather be maintained, though corrected and reassessed as regards its rhythms of development and its modalities of functioning. Durkheim mostly accepts the division of labor and the process of industrialization of a capitalist type as a minor evil or perhaps as a certainly problematical situation, but one still susceptible to positive measures to correct it. In fact, in Durkheim one does not see the pungent criticisms, at times ruthless, which at times, from Marx and Proudhon to the Frankfurt School, are a basic drive. In Durkheim, industrial society is not a polemical object, but something to be achieved. The division of labor itself, far from being in itself an evil, is presented as the condition for the rise of a more advanced form of solidarity—the "organic." In fact, he recognizes only two forms of solidarity, the "mechanical," which directly binds the individual to society without intermediaries, and the "organic" in which the individual instead depends on society because he depends on the parts which make it up. However, solidarity always needs "rules." In the *Social Division of Labor*, Durkheim insists on a basic postulate: the lack of regulation does not allow the regular harmony of functions. An example of this crisis of anomie (literally, the absence of laws) is provided by the relations between capital and labor, relations which, in his view, have remained in a state of juridical indeterminacy. But where does this state originate? Durkheim asks. The answer is obvious: as a body of rules is the definitive form in which through time relations between social functions are spontaneously established, one may say that, a priori, the state of anomie is impossible wherever the organs of solidarity are sufficiently and long enough in contact. Hence it is clear that Durkheim's proposed solution for the crisis of industrial society must be sought in the "corporation," once an elementary division of communal organization and in Durkheim's view now destined to become the elementary division of the state, the basic political unit.

Here, the lack of a perspective concerning social change and economic development weighs heavily on Durkheim's thought to the point of entering a clearly one-way street. The conflict of interests, which can be a powerful mainspring for any society, is here softened and regulated to the point of its suffocation in such a sociocentric structure that one cannot see how ultimately it could avoid presenting itself as an authoritarian one. However, this critical complaint, well founded though I think it is, does not damage the coherence of Durkheim's theoretical system. This system hinges on solidarity as a manifestation of society, not only as mechanical "togetherness" or one of dynamically opposing forces, but primarily as "the only moral personality to be found above particular personalities," and as such able to impose itself on individuals, being endowed with the continuity and even the lasting quality necessary to maintain order, over and above the ephemeral relations which flesh it out in everyday life.

SOCIAL COHESION AS AN OPEN PROBLEM

The research on suicide and the religious life in this perspective are compulsory themes, areas to which Durkheim is attached and which he deals with in full, conscious awareness. Suicide, an act erroneously believed to be individual, is a valuable indicator of the diminution of the cohesion of the social group to which one belongs. There are no suicides—only persons who have been "suicided." In this, Durkheim's argument is tight. Working on secondary data, mostly official statistics, he notes that the suicide rate is significantly correlated with the type and degree of social cohesion. In this sense, it is a socially determined act, for which a purely psychologico-individual explanation does not suffice. After distinguishing two types of suicide, the egoistical and the altruistic. Durkheim goes on to consider a third type, defined as "anomic," which is an important contribution to sociological theory. He departs from the argument that poverty in itself cannot be considered an important determinant of suicide: indeed, the data show that the reverse is true. But then, he argues, if poverty protects one from suicide, it is a sign that it is in itself a brake. However it is done, desires are to a certain extent forced to come to terms with means available, and what one has serves partly as a reference point to determine what one would like. Thus, the less one has, the less one is led to enlarge infinitely the circle of needs. On the other hand, the less one feels limited, the more intolerable every limitation appears. It is not unreasonable, he remarks in passing, that so many religions have celebrated the blessings and moral value of poverty. He concludes: "If anomy . . . appeared . . . [only] in intermittent spurts and acute crisis, it might cause the suicide rate to vary from time to time, but it would not be a regular, constant factor. In one sphere of social life, however—the sphere of trade and industry—it is actually in a chronic state."[6] Here we see fully the deeply conservative orientation of Durkheim. "[R]eligion . . . has lost most of its power. And government, instead of regulating economic life, has become its tool and servant. The most opposite schools, orthodox economists and extreme socialists, unite to reduce government to the role of a more or less passive intermediary among the various social functions. . . . But both refuse it any power to subordinate other social organs to itself and to make them converge toward one dominant aim."[7] But again, his thought is presented with his characteristic ambivalence. There is, in his conservative orientation, still living a radical critique against the individualistic utilitarianism which recognizes no other basis of social legitimacy beyond the individual's egoism. The "displacement of ends" means the transformation of those which, by principle, should be only instruments into social ends: this does not escape Durkheim: "And as these theories merely express the state of opinion, industry instead of being still regarded as a means to an end transcending itself, has become the supreme end of individuals and societies alike. Thereupon, the appetites thus excited have become freed of any limiting authority. By sanctifying them, so to speak, this apotheosis of wellbeing has placed them above all human law. Their restraint seems like a sort of sacrilege. For this reason, even the purely utilitarian regulation of them exercised by the industrial world itself through the medium of occupational groups has been unable to persist. Ultimately, this liberation of desires has been made worse by the very development of industry and the almost infinite extension of the market."[8]

The fall in standards of judgment and "social constraints" is thus for Durkheim at the basis of the increase of suicides. Suicide is thus essentially a social fact, as much as is religious life. For Durkheim a religion is a solidarist system of beliefs and practices related to things that are sacred, or set apart. Such a system unites its adherents into a single moral community called a church. The source of the sacred is thus in society, since the idea of religion is inseparable from that of church; thus it becomes clear that religion is preeminently a collective matter. It would thus seem that, to Durkheim, there could be no religious life outside a formal social organization, and that thus religion is necessarily church religion and not also religiosity, to be understood as the intimate internal experience of the individual.[9]

NOTES

1. E. Durkheim, *Le socialisme: sa définition, ses débuts, la doctrine saint-simonienne*, Paris: F. Alcan, 1928; cited from the Italian tran.: *Il socialismo*, trans. by E. Roggero, Milano: F. Angeli, 1973, p. 370.

2. Durkheim, *Le socialisme*, p. 370.

3. E. Durkheim, *La science sociale et l'action*, Paris: Presses Universitaires de France, 1970; cited from the Italian tran.: *La scienza sociale e l'azione*, trans. by S. Veca, Milano: Il Saggiatore, 1972, pp. 261–71.

4. See A. Izzo's "Introduzione" to *Antologia di scritti sociologici Durkheim*, Bologna: Il Mulino, 1978, p. 19.

5. Izzo, "Introduzione," p. 19.

6. E. Durkheim, *Suicide*, trans. by J.A. Spaulding and G. Simpson, New York: Free Press, 1951, p. 254.

7. Durkheim, *Suicide*, p. 255.

8. Durkheim, *Suicide*, p. 255.

9. Cf. my study "Il destino della ragione e il paradosso del sacro," *La Critica Sociologica*, n. 47, 1971.

6

+

Max Weber: The Orphan of Bismarck and the Crisis of European Society

A PARTICULAR SOCIOLOGIST, THOUGH WITH A RETICENCE OF COMMITMENT

Max Weber has been long and minutely studied by sociologists, but also by historians, students of methodology, economics, and jurisprudence. A central figure in the scientific debate of the first half of the twentieth century, he is in fact located at the intersection of various, different disciplines and intellectual viewpoints; his thought rapidly assumed the function of a mediating filter which was critico-problematic at the same time. It is odd, given this position as witness and protagonist of the crisis, that Max Weber should have been capable of being presented as the champion of "value-freedom," as the exponent and author of a neutral aseptic social science, dumb in the face of the essential values and problems, which from the first years of this century, were shaking European society to its foundations.

As did other important scholars of European social problems (for example, Karl Mannheim, Vilfredo Pareto, Roberto Michels, and Durkheim as well), Max Weber too returned to Europe after passing through the United States. This was not a painless passage: it meant for Weber the loss of his characteristic pathos regarding the great problems. After all, after the philological and hermeneutic attentions of Talcott Parsons and Edward A. Shils, Weber returned to Europe much more photogenic but smoothed out and softened, and basically poorer both conceptually and humanly. The man who endured problems to the point of pain with direct and obvious impact on his private life—so much so as to have to leave regular teaching in the university to return home and reduce himself to the position of German *Privat-Gelehrter*—was made to pass for the implacable analyst who preached absolute objectivity in the name of pure, distanced science. Nothing is further from the truth. This presentation possibly demonstrates, and was determined by, a double aim: in the first place, to convert the complex and problematic figure of Max Weber and, by mutilating and simplifying it, to reduce its stature to the point of making it a simple pioneer—a kind of first step on the road which was to lead to the construction of Talcott Parsons's "social system." Second, it was intended to produce a real intellectual embargo against the presence and influence of the thought of Karl Marx, which, on the contrary, had obsessed and followed like a tormenting shadow the intellectual itinerary and development of Weber for his whole life.

In fact, for years Weber was embalmed, and his basic intention misconceived. Far from being a cold and distant analyst, Weber—while maintaining his reticence of commitment—immersed himself in and directly confronted the social and political problems of his time. What he did not tolerate was that it was possible to pass off as results of scientific research, hence beyond any possibility of doubt and dispute, what were rather merely personal opinions, if not downright prejudices. What Weber feared and what he assailed was the improper use of the university position to diffuse as scientific truths purely personal ideas and interpretations. Naturally, he had in mind colleagues: for example, the nationalist "Treitschkes" (so-named for the nationalist and anti-Semitic historian Heinrich von Treitschke).

In addition, it is enough to make a list of the developing themes of Weber's reflection and his scientific work to realize how committed he was. These are the relation between ethics and economic activity, especially between the Protestant ethic and the birth of the capitalist spirit—a major theme, for whose demonstration Weber was to undertake the mighty historico-comparative researches into universal religions. Then there are the methodological discussions concerning the convergences and basic differences between the sciences of nature and the social sciences, or "culture," as Weber preferred to call them; discussions which were to lead him to a position equally distant from historicism and positivism. Next there is the problem of the "dominant variable," the variable with priority, which Weber managed to demonstrate clearly, and wherein he criticized Marxism, which in his view tended to favor one level—the economico-structural one—as regards the other political, ideological, and juridical levels of society. He investigated the forms of power and their evolution through history from the traditional-patriarchal to the bureaucratic-legal and the charismatic-prophetic. Finally, he dealt with the question of the rationalization of industrial society and the arrival of a "disenchanted world."

A RELUCTANT NATIONALIST

Just as it is difficult and in my view impossible to define Weber as a "neutral" sociologist with that indifference which inevitably accompanies this well-deserved title, the question of the politically open character of his social and intellectual position is equally difficult, as it emerges not only from his systematic and scientific writings but also from his abundant contributions to reviews and newspapers close to current events. As his mentor Theodor Mommsen said of him, Weber remained a political animal, even if as a politician manqué. The failure of Weber as a politician was certainly also due to the characteristics of the political life and the structures and methods of functioning of the political organisms of his time. However, it is not only ascribable to this. In Weber there were uncertainties and ambiguities which he did not know how, or did not wish ever, to overcome. Wolfgang Mommsen's *Max Weber und die deutsche Politik, 1890–1920* provided perhaps the most accurate monograph on Weber the politician. According to his interpretation, one must see in Weber one who consciously anticipated chauvinism and imperialism. In his view, although Weber never lost the opportunity to attack the Kaiser and Chancellor Bismarck, his politics never went beyond a more or less paternalistic nationalism. As I have observed elsewhere, according to Mommsen Weber composed a sociology of force imbued with such a basic pessimism as to recall Machiavelli and Hobbes. Furthermore, he conceived of law as a purely rational and formal end, without even the suspicion that the constitutionally guaranteed limitation of force and its use could at times be very important, if not decisive. In a word, Weber places himself on the same level as Nietzsche by reason of his fanaticism for the transcendental, charismatic dictatorship.

Clearly, this is a polemical and extreme interpretation. It is, however, incontrovertible that Weber essentially remains a nationalist who understood the problems of institutional political development and economic development as functions of national interests. In his theoretical political thought and sociological research, in that they present powerful critical cases against the bureaucratic regimes of the Wilhelmine era, it is certainly possible to see the embryonic elements of a theory of "guided democracy of a plebicitory type." However, Weber continually and coherently said that this was inapplicable to the German nation, which in his view would not have the tendency to understand and translate into political practice popular sovereignty, because it lacked the basic historical experience of rebellion against its ruler.[1]

Though in bitterest polemic against the Junkers and their agrarian policy, and against the liberals, their natural allies, in the face of the danger presented by the Social-Democrats, Weber did not manage to convince himself to accept the positions of the latter, whom he always held to be "politically immature." This in Weberian terms means incapable of understanding the function of violence in the development of historical forces and unable to understand and appropriate the logic of power. While fiercely criticizing the Crown, and under the pressure of a widespread leftism, especially lively among the students, it is clear that Weber did not believe in democracy as such—that is, in the intrinsic validity of the system. But he admitted it only insofar as it could possibly provide efficient political leaders capable of taking on responsibilities for command, instead of carrying on corridor politics in the imperial antechambers.

Certainly, in his critical attitude toward formal democracy, there is the imprint of a Marxist influence—but this is a shadow. What seems characteristic of Weber is in fact this strange salamander property, which allowed him to pass unharmed through the fires of opposing ideologies and which prevented him from becoming a "true believer," an *engagé*, and which indeed paralyzed him when there was a question of making that "intellectual sacrifice" which is the going price of any faith, of any closed ideological system. However, it was the political struggle with the sacrifices also, if not mainly, intellectual, which it requires, which attracted him violently. In him, two powerful tendencies are continually at work, contrary and simultaneous, which lacerated him: the need for intellectual clarity, and the sense, almost the physical taste, of power, of force, of the decision which cuts short and settles.

CHARISMA AS AN IRRATIONALIST TEMPTATION IN A PERIOD OF CRISIS

The charismatic leader is the conceptual instrument and the existential stratagem for the resolution of the nodal point, of this wound which, for him, right to the end, bleeds. Notwithstanding the flexibility of its duration, linked to the fate of the individual, in Weber charismatic power plays a decisive role. It breaks the bureaucratic routine, it revives (as he points out in *Politik als Beruf*) the moribund bureaucratic regime by referring it back to the profundity of that mysterious, contradictory, and fascinating forbidden game, which for Weber is politics. We think we can understand the situation within which Weber moves and thinks: the excruciating contradiction between the appeal to the miraculous activist fever of the demiurgic will which directs peoples and makes history, and the quiet, rational twilight calm of the perfect academic and that of the Herr Professor *malgré lui*. We understand that as a young boy he astounded his mother, as Marianne Weber tells us,[2] by severely condemning in Cicero a politician of limited abilities, who was content to be an "irresponsible orator" instead of presenting himself as a true leader: as Gramsci would say, as a "permanent persuader." However, the real reason for Weber's rejection of Cicero is different and meaningful. Weber condemns Cicero for his ambiguous behavior as regards Cataline, whose conspiracy the young Weber would not have hesitated to suppress violently. He was to write toward the end of *Politik als Beruf* that the devil of politics and the God of love are in intimate mutual struggle. I think I understand Weber's difficult position: on the one hand he does not feel able to make the "intellectual sacrifice" for ideological belief; on the other, he does not manage to establish a logical and continual relation between intellectual clarity and political decisions, between human needs inductively (scientifically) established and power. One might say that his faith, which is "visceral" in the "masses" of the base, essentially cuts off any exit. There is open to him only the dubious path of Titanism, the road of the prophet and the charismatic leader. Human destiny returns to the inscrutable hands of the gods. Charismatic power is thus a moment of rupture, the factor of change par excellence, revolutionary and out of the ordinary; but at the same time it is by definition irrational, a mysterious gift of divine origin (*gottgesandt*), but at least such as to present itself as an example to be followed (*vorbildlich*). Weber is perfectly aware that the notion of charisma has a religious origin. Perhaps more alertly than elsewhere, in his introduction to the essays on *Religionssoziologie* Weber made it clear that charisma refers to an extraordinary personal quality, whether the person is real or not. Charismatic authority means domination, whether more internal or external, over men and women, to which they submit because of their faith in the quality possessed by this specific person. The shaman, the prophet, the warrior, and so on, and in certain circumstances the personal party leader, are types of rulers that are counterposed to their respective groups. The legitimacy of their rule is based on faith and dedication to what goes beyond the ordinary. To what, in fact, is appreciated because it surpasses normal human qualities.

The religious origin of the idea of charisma is obviously taken for granted. It is well known that when writing about the charismatic leader, Weber is thinking of the Old Testament Prophet. So it is interesting to note that Pauline charisms are also gratuitous, supernatural graces, impermanent, and bestowed for general usefulness.

It is clear that charismatic power, seemingly strong, indeed divine, is really fragile, because, as an attribute of the individual, it cannot be transmitted and is a part of historical exception. The most solid power is certainly the traditional—patriarchal—one, based on the authority of the eternal yesterday—that is to say, on the authority of tradition and customs. However, the typical power of an industrializing society, or of bourgeois society, is bureaucratic legal power with its impersonal norms and depersonalized responsibilities, perfectly routinized. Weber's attitude is quite ambivalent. On the one hand, he understands that the spirit of capitalism and the rationality which characterizes it need this regular, foreseeable ordered and formally legal power. On the other, Weber almost instinctively fears that bureaucratic power, with its formal rationality, might end up by killing life just as Nietzsche was afraid that the pedantic concern of the philologists might prevent one from understanding the genuine spirit of the Greek classics by counting Homer's commas—forgetting the essence of the way of life which still was unaware of the schism between body and spirit introduced by Christianity.

It is clear that these "pure" types of power (traditional bureaucratic-legal and charismatic) are only, in Weber's terminology, "ideal types," that is, modes of behavior drawn from the analysis of historical material, but which are basically analytical and should not be confused with specific historical contents. They help to direct research. As parameters, they indicate how effective, inductively (historically) ascertained behavior deviates from or converges on the "ideal-type."

BUREAUCRATIC POWER IS CONSTITUTIONALLY INCAPABLE OF CONFRONTING THE CRISIS

The clarity with which Weber saw the contemporary problems of Germany, the poverty and mediocrity of its political managers at a moment when, with the industrialization of the country and the growth of its economic power, the need for a general, rational political management became more pressing and urgent, is truly impressive. Weber understood that the spirit of capitalism did not lie in the *auri sacra fames*, or simply in the reinvestment of purloined capital, but rather in rational calculation, in the ability to connect the desired ends with the available means, with the active presence of a ruling class freed from the ancestral dreams of the medieval night, sober, lucid, and rationally pragmatic. This ruling class did not exist in Germany. Weber's polemic against the invasion of parliament by state bureaucrats and functionaries rests precisely on the basic argument that the spirit of the bureaucrat lies in obeying formal rules, in waiting for promotion due to length of service, and that this is the sure way to extinguish any ability to take political responsibility in the real sense, any ability to lead, decide, govern—that is, to make a choice. It has been correctly noted that "what appeared immediately obvious to Weber, to the extent of considering it the most significant fact of post-Bismarckian Germany, is the indisputable fact of its political instability. . . . What Weber charges Bismarck with, and was to do so with ever-increasing emphasis, what represented the most negative aspect of his use of power and the effects of which continued to be influential in a restrictive way, even after his fall, was to have impeded the formation not only of a consciousness but above all specifically bourgeois apparatuses. That is, institutional structures around which the emerging class of the industrial bourgeoisie might have grouped their forces as a means of strategy on the political level still more than on the level of ideas, so as to oppose the challenge that historical social democracy was launching at that time."[3]

Weber's anxious predictions concerning the rationalizing and bureaucratizing tendencies of the whole of society—political professionalism increasingly tied to business matters and mediocrity, the inadequacy of European leadership regarding the real, functional problems and of direction of the new industrial mass societies—were essentially confirmed. In fact, the problem posed by bureaucratization does not only concern capitalist societies but also those described as societies of "real socialism," in which a ponderous bureaucratic structure seems to cover an actual state of anarchy.

A PECULIAR BLINDNESS

Against this extraordinary clairvoyance there remains a disturbing question. How was it that Weber did not manage to predict the coming of Marxism? and indeed that by having the famous Article 4B inserted into the Weimar Constitution (also known as the *Diktatur* paragraph) by which, in exceptional situations, full powers go to the Reichspräsident, he made himself an unconscious accomplice of Hitler, who, thanks to that article, was able legally to take power?

From this question, one must begin a critical, double argument, both on Weber's methodology and on his social origins and the limits those origins directly or indirectly imposed on him. One of Weber's great merits was the global formulation of sociological research, beyond any fragmentary specialization which might impede a view of the problem in its total significance. Having said this, one must however recognize that Weber's globality is static. The components of the social are all in context, and coordinatedly investigated. But there is a refusal to give them differential value, with the inevitable result of a stasis which implies the inexplicability of the historic process as a dynamic process under development. In Weber, these limitations fuse with social conditioning. This point has not always been grasped, even by well-informed and acute analysts. For example, W. G. Runciman carefully limits his critical questionings to the internal characteristics of Weber's scheme.[4]

However, so close is the tie in Weber between reflection on methodology and research on specific themes that even a critique in deliberately formalistic terms like Runciman's ends up plumbing the depths of essential problems. Runciman finds Weber wrong on three points: a) he does not grasp the difference between theoretical assumptions and implicit value judgments; b) the way in which "ideographic" explanations are incorporated into the framework of causal laws is not clear to him; c) he did not correctly understand the relationship between explanation and description. In particular, Runciman complains that by maintaining a qualitative difference between social sciences and sciences of nature, Weber made too many concessions to the idealists while openly refusing to bridge the abyss which, in the latter's view, was supposed to divide dichotomously the field of sciences between ineffable spirit and standardizing laws. In reality, it seems to me that Runciman wants very simply and rather hurriedly to carry Weber into the embrace of Popper, with the sole exception of expressing wonder because of the lasting validity and indeed growing interest of Weber's methodological and substantial teaching. However, the reason, which is not a chance one, for this lasting validity is precisely to be sought in the fact that Weber is placed and indeed—as I have elsewhere noted—inserts himself into the heart of the problematic tension running between positivism and historicism. The former is the tendency to consider human facts, which are always historical facts, as purely material realities, "factual"— *things*, as Durkheim said—and the opposite tendency which saw in human fact something ineffable, a real reality but an intimate and mysterious one which one could only "relive" and experience personally but not positively analyze so as to arrive at a public knowledge and explanation—that is, an intersubjective one, verifiable by everyone.

I would say that Runciman does not wholly take into account the fact that for Weber historical awareness necessarily involves the rejection of the search for absolute, nontemporal truths, and for this basic reason it never sets itself to the building of an all-encompassing system. However much social and natural sciences may converge, even to the point of coinciding, it seems to me difficult that Weber's reservation concerning the specific character of "human motivation" at work in society as compared with biological or physical research, for example, loses its importance and can be lightly ignored. What it seems to me that Runciman sees very well is Weber's individualism, a "methodological individualism" which according to Runciman allows Weber to anticipate by nearly forty years the recent arguments of Popper and his followers, especially in England, and which is based on the assertion that "propositions which employ collective concepts can be verified only by reference to individual behavior."[5] It is useless to speak of the polemical confrontation which this position involves for Durkheim—one, however, never directly mentioned by Weber. Rather, one should point out here how the peculiar contradiction into which Weber falls in this regard escapes Runciman. The great scholar of the great historical subjects—capitalism, Christianity, and so on—and structural social situations, runs the risk of losing his own analyses in the purely relational and motivational fluxes of the most old-fashioned psychologism.

Here, Weber's social origin and political choice may play a determining role. They release his value-premises and principles of personal preference which are purely elitist. Although the matter is not scientifically demonstrable and is logically absurd, from the point of view of the apparatus of Weber's work, his methodological individualism necessarily leads to a societal nominalism without exit, as though man and his interests and his individual motivation had in them their justification and explanatory key. This is not only a question of method: it involves problems of substance. In Weber's case methodological individualism and political elitism go hand in hand. Vittorio Saltini has drawn attention to what he calls an undue emphasis on my part of Weber's elitism.[6] In this regard, he notes that Weber, "after all, fought for universal suffrage, union freedom, and for the collective contract of labor." There is no doubt about the liberal spirit of Weber. However, faced with an emergency situation, when in the institutional fabric of representative liberal democracy with a relatively narrow social base, there opened up obvious cracks and it was no longer possible with the means and methods of normal administration to withstand the growing demand for participation which arose from the base, the conditioned reflex to which Weber succumbed was that of the strong man. He looked for the charismatic leader who emerges in the great historical crises as the supreme restorer, the new leadership—in order that the base does not move and so that the leaders do not have to tremble more than necessary. It is clear that Weber did not fall into the vulgar commonplaces which were to become popularized—as regards the problem of efficient and open leadership—by the legion of neopluralists, from James Burnham to Schumpeter, concerned to empty the concept of democracy so as to reduce it to a simple procedural device. Weber was too alert and morally too exceptional not to be aware that to reduce the problem of the historic test of democracy to the competitive alternation between different elites fighting for power would lower and narrow the concept of democracy to the point where it meant choosing between nominally alternative but really equivalent slaveries. He stopped in front of the dilemma—either *Führerdemocratie*, that is, democracy held from above, or the fall into *camarilla*. He did not see, could not see, a way out in a democracy with a broader social base, certainly problematic and difficult, but to be attempted. Saltini remarks that "in the Utopian and Marxist idea of the transcendence of formal rationality in collective participation . . . there is an anti-pluralist, totalitarian claim."[7] This danger is real but I ask myself if, by hiding behind it, we can close our eyes to the pseudo-pluralism which has voided popular sovereignty of any meaning so as to eternalize as a *ne plus ultra* of humanity's development what is simply a specific phase of its evolution.

NOTES

1. Concerning the theoretical and practical difficulties of the democratic regime in Germany, cf. Ralf Dahrendorf's *Gesellschaft und Freiheit, zur soziologischen Analyse der Regenwart*, Munich: R. Piper, 1962, especially "Demokratie und Sozialstruktur in Deutschland," pp. 260–300. The attempts at psychological and sociological explanation by Erich Fromm and Th. W. Adorno are well known.

2. Cf. Marianne Weber, *Max Weber: ein Lebensbild*, Heidelberg: L. Schneider, 1950.

3. Cf. A. Roversi, *Max Weber e la sociologia della crisi*, in *La Critica Sociologica*, n. 43, 1977, p. 132.

4. Cf. W. G. Runciman, *A Critique of Max Weber's Philosophy of Social Science*, Cambridge, Eng.: Cambridge Univ. Press, 1972.

5. Runciman, *A Critique*, p. 24.

6. Cf. V. Saltini, "I pericoli della dialettica," in *L'Espresso*, 29 February 1973.

7. Cf. V. Saltini, "L'uomo di fronte al potere," in *L'Espresso*, 4 March 1973.

7

✛

Georg Simmel: The Forms of Social Relations and Objectified Spirit

A RADICAL QUESTIONING

Though connected in various ways for many years with the German university world, it is hard to see Georg Simmel as a normal academic. The man was too lively, sensitive, spiritually mobile, and unprejudiced, too "catholic" in the etymological meaning of the word[1] as regards human and scientific interests, not to cast off its restraints. It was impossible to enclose him in the formal framework of a bureaucratic-professional set of rules. In the very field of sociological research and meditation, his was a position to one side; it marked a "separate vocation," outside the line and traditions of the great schools. In that his position was similar to—though in a quite different social and cultural environment—the bitter and lonely position of a Thorstein Veblen.

Simmel went off on his own. He did not ask himself what the nature of society was, what the dynamics of the social process and the "laws" of its dynamic development were. He posed a much more radical question: *how is society possible?* The reply to this question, which lies at the basis of any sociology, was not formulated in a precise and unequivocal way, but the merit of asking it explicitly and precisely so as to make it a preliminary, unavoidable problem, is all his. Add to this the extraordinary breadth of cultural references, which runs from sociology to history, philosophy, art, and literature, the swift, brilliant nature of the style, worthy in parts of the best French essayist and unequaled in German culture save for some work by Benjamin and Adorno, the intuitive and at the same time rigorous progression of his thoughts, and one will easily understand why his work is a necessary passage (though little traveled) for the construction of the science of society, and, at the same time, fascinating reading.

Preparing to enlarge upon the reply to the question of the "possibility of society," Simmel set up a bold comparison with Kant's question on the "possibility of nature." Simmel makes it clear that Kant could pose the question only because nature was the same as the "representation of nature" (*die Vorstellung der Natur*).[2]

What does this mean? What means the statement that one can respond to the question "how is nature possible" only by *reducing* nature to its own "representation"? Does this perhaps mean that nature is possible only because it is already present in us, as an "internal object of our consciousness" (*ein Inhalt unseres Bewusstseins*)? Simmel's reply, speaking here with Kant's voice, is in equilibrium between naturalistic objectivism and psychologizing subjectivism. There is no doubt that this involves high intellectual acrobatics, not without methodological and essential risks, but suggestive. The data of nature arrive by chance, as disconnected perceptions, fragmentary in themselves, and are thus not yet "nature" in themselves. They become it, however, through the filter of knowledge—what Simmel calls, somewhat equivocally, "the activity of the spirit" (*die Aktivität des Geistes*). I observe that for Simmel as for Kant, who acts here as spokesman, this activity is not so much "creative" as an "organizing" activity. It guarantees the "binding" (*Verbingung*) which connects and unifies data—that is, those fragments of the world, incoherent in themselves and with no necessary interrelations, which as a whole, and only as meaningful whole, make up nature.

Simmel asks himself if one should not analogously tackle the problem of the makeup of society. Are there not perhaps here also isolated individuals, separate perceptions, which are waiting to be consciously organized into a globality? However, an immediate qualitative distinction between nature and society is at once established by Simmel. Nature for Kant is constituted only in the observing subject: it is in the subject that it finds its "unity" in the true sense. In the case of society, things are quite different. The individual observers are not the decisive elements since society has its autonomous and internal dynamic, in that its unity is determined by its own elements, which are not passive "data," but rather conscious and capable of synthetic activity (*bewusst und synthetisch-aktiv*). This apparatus of reasoning, which recalls the typical ability of the subject to create vital interconnections between the elements of experience so as to be able to relive past experience (the famous *Erlebnis*) is a basic leitmotiv of German thought and returns continually to mark the qualitative difference between the human world and the natural environemnt, and hence between the sciences of nature and those of history, or culture. Historically, it was Weber who overcame this hiatus, which also marked a traditional limitation of the social sciences in Germany. However, Simmel already took the first important steps in the right direction: "Kant's formula: a connection can never be given in things, as it comes into being only through the subject, it does not hold good for the social nexus which is established much more immediately in the 'things,' which in this case are individual souls."[3]

SOCIETY AS AN OBJECTIVE UNITY

Furthermore, society is an objective unity and exists as an interindividual relation, whether or not this is studied or observed. Society is thus a unique globality, with characteristics which can be much more intimate—such as love, understanding the affective ties between human beings—than are the objects of nature in space, or the globality which is the natural reality of a table, a chair. At the same time they have more fluid, dramatic characteristics, because they are not statistically fixed once for all. Finally, for Simmel the problem of whether society is possible has a completely different methodical sense as regards the question: how is nature possible? This awareness of the difference for him lies in the last resort in the different role played by the observer as regards nature and society. To know nature, the subject filters, unifies, and organizes the fragmentary, unconnected data of sensory experience. When we are dealing with society, the subject does not know by counterposing himself to a reality, but rather learns to know by participating in the reality he would like to know: that is, he knows by being at once analyst and participant, critically distanced but also emotively involved. Indeed, "the subject is not here up against an object, from which he draws a theoretical image, but rather it is precisely that awareness of socialization which is immediately his support (*Träger*) or interior meaning (*innere Bedeutung*)."[4] It is incredible that such intuitions should have been allowed to die or that at least they have been passed over in silence by historians of sociology. Not only is there already here in embryo a picture of what we have elsewhere called "sociology as participation," but one can also grasp the elements basic to a construction of an epistemological model of the social sciences, and thus of a methodology, which may locate itself outside the prevailing mechanistic models. These models are responsible for the formulation of theories and sociological methods which are at once technically refined and without human significance.

The simplifications Simmel offers are always suggestive, but at times are fleeting, more metaphorical than empirically verifiable. Moreover, he recognizes and never tires of repeating that it is not possible to express his conceptions "in one word," like Kant, and perhaps here one should say that his modesty points to a defect. He finds himself forced to construct typ-ical situations—a few years later Weber was to call them "ideal-typical"—from which the reader can extract what the author means, in conditions of greater comprehensibility.

The first example concerns the social relationship: that is, the relation of the subject with another or, if you will, the image a man makes of another because of a personal relation. Though indeed we are dealing with a per-sonal relation, Simmel tried to show that this image is not direct; on the contrary, it is inevitably mediated by social perspectives and the fact that necessarily the relation takes place in society. Of all the human beings liv-ing together in society, no one can know the other in a direct, exhaustive fashion, completely outside social determinants. That is only possible—but even then only partly—in relations of intimate friendship, when, for him, the relation is dominated by "similarity" (*Gleichheit*) between two souls.

It does not seem too clear here whether Simmel was thinking of Plato's *Phaedrus* where the latter says that the friend cannot even see and understand himself except when reflected in his friend's eye, or if he tended instead to anticipate George Herbert Mead's concept of the "generalized other," the midpoint and crossover between the strictly (idiosyncratically) individual and the socioinstitutional, whether or not formally codified. It is certain that in his view "in order to know man, we do not see him according to his pure individuality, but rather as rep-resented, elevated or lowered on the basis of the general type under which we catalogue him."[5]

THE CONCEPT OF SOCIAL ROLE

Thus for Simmel, the concept of social role emerges as the sociological-formal parallel to the breakup of the social framework which historically occurred on a vast scale through the industrial revolution by way of the social division of labor, with its consequent specialization of tasks and professionalization of functions. As regards this specific demonstration of the results to which his formal sociological method leads, Simmel's words reach a remarkable level of suggestiveness, which may perhaps justify the label at times given to him (moreover, also by Weber) of the "sociologist of decadence." He said, "We are all fragments [*Wir alle sind Fragmente*] not only of general man, but rather also of ourselves. We are slivers [*Ansätze*] not only as regards the man-type in general, not only as regards good and evil, and so on, but also as regards the individuality and singularity—in principle no longer definable—of ourselves, whose individuality and sin-gularity surround, as though sketched out by ideal lines, our perceptible reality."[6] In fact, he explained, we see the other no more as a simple individual, but rather on the basis of a series of social determinations, which are roles, or part of a couple we all play in life. We see the other as a colleague at work, at the office, at a party, as a professional of a certain type, a member of a certain professional category. In reality, therefore, we do not see the other as an other, but rather that part of the other which allows us to glimpse the social role, the label behind which he hides his real individuality, which in its unique, irreducible, unrepeatable reality remains an unknown country, mysterious, and wholly to be discovered. Thus he concluded, "in the representation of man, the individual finds displacements, detractions, integrations (as generalization is always at the same time that of individuality, more or less), derived from all the *a priori* categories: from his type as a man, the notion of his own fulfillment in terms of success, and the social generality to which he belongs. On all this there floats, as the heuristic principle of knowing, the idea of his real, indeterminate individual significance; although, however, it seems that only the attainment of this indeterminacy could give us the really fundamental relation for knowledge of those changes and images [*jene Veränderungen und Neugestaltungen*] which prevent this ideal knowledge, and precisely the conditions [*Bedingung*]through which there become possible the relations which we alone know as social."[7]

Naturally, things would be simpler if the individual stuck completely to and thus fulfilled the social role assigned to him. Instead, Simmel notes, "every element of a group is not only part of society, but furthermore something else again."[8] Here indeed one finds the roots of the drama of the individual in society. The subject goes beyond his social determinateness, and crosses the socially established frontiers of his acknowledged role. This friction, indeed this contradiction, cannot only be expressed in terms of maladaptation to the role. Everyone knows there are fathers not adapted to assume the responsibility and duties of fatherhood, or the lawyer who is destined to remain without clients because he prefers literature and literary discussions to the articles of the civil and penal codes. But it is not only this. There are real role contradictions which clash in the individual and torment his vital experience. To quote a now classic case, think of the mother who did not want to renounce realizing herself in a personal career outside the family. The expectations of role and the characteristics of the two social positions are so differentiated, both practically and in the common perception of people, as to become rapidly antithetical and at times self-exclusive. The subject who lives through them can be split to the point of neurosis, if not schizophrenia. I have the impression that Simmel only considers the problem of that part of the individual which is not involved and thus not absorbed by society, then remaining simply "without relations" (*beziehungslos*) with respect to the socially meaningful part. To him, this creates a dialectical relation between the part, and the way in which the subject is socialized, and the other part which expresses his way of not being socialized.

THE RELATIVE AUTONOMY OF THE INDIVIDUAL

Simmel's thesis is that one cannot really participate, that is, as subject, in the full sense, in social life unless one reserves for oneself the part which is not resolved, not dissolved in society. I think I may add: because one can participate in society, as in other realities, only to the extent that one exists as relatively autonomous. For Simmel, the social role has meaning and can be lived humanly only if the human subject preserves a life for himself, a nonsocialized part of himself. We know, he elaborated, of the clerk that he is not only a clerk, and of the shopkeeper that he is not only a shopkeeper, and of the official—and so on: individuals, as the professions and social situations, are distinguished on the basis of the level of the "beyond" they possess, or permit, along with their social content. He discovered here and set out the essence of the problematic situation which Lionel Trilling was to call the question of the Opposing Self, a typically modern question, which arises when the individual no longer sticks to, nor only expresses himself in, his publicly determined social role, or when modern society begins to open up relatively autonomous spaces to the initiatives of the subject, and thus presents itself as "civil society."

Simmel, however, had his eye above all on that part of the personal which could still express itself within the social role. In other words, while recognizing the inevitability and legitimacy—from the point of view of social life—of the existence of fixed roles categorized on the basis of the needs of the social system, he seemed to ask for "supplement of soul," as it were, or a personalization of the role to the extent this would be possible without harming the interests of impersonally organized social life. In reality, in the social conditions determined by capitalism social roles can be lived by the subject with a very reduced level of individual creativity. The "money economy," as Simmel usually calls it, is certainly not tender in this respect. On the other hand, this economy characterizes all modern culture, and it is precisely in this culture, he noted, that man as producer, buyer, or seller, or generally as subject of some output (*als irgendein Leistender*), approaches the ideal of absolute objectivity.

It is incredible that here, independently of empirical field research and by pure introspection, and thus on a purely intuitive basis, Simmel should have been able to anticipate the analysis of the social and psychic effects of bureaucratization which were to have in Weber their more profound and comprehensive analyst, and which were to allow also the description and explanation of the mechanism of the process of rationalizing social life as a meta-ideological process, in the exact sense that it passes beneath the contrasting ideologies and concerns basically both capitalism and socialism. "Men become simply the bearers of an education between fulfilment and counterfulfillment [*Leistung und Gegenleistung*], which takes place according to objective norms."[9] Here we touch upon the element, perhaps the most meaningful, of the dramatic position of man in the world—the incomplete capacity of fulfilling the subject in his social activity. The individual soul can never remain within a tie if at the same time it does not stand outside it. It cannot be rooted in any order without at the same time rising up against it.[10]

There is more. We have already presented here the form of the basic arguments which will be found in the admirable *Philosophie des Geldes*. Not only this, but Simmel here anticipates, with extraordinary clarity and precision the essence of the criticisms of society and mass culture set out later by the Frankfurt School, especially Adorno and Horkheimer. The crisis of a "wholly administered" world, one thus unable to respect the essential instant of the "involuntariness of thought," and even to recognize a non-marked, unpredictable "extra-territoriality" in the individual's most intimate feelings, is already radically explained here and warned against. Not even the religious man, he said, can totally negate himself in the existence of God, by feeling himself no more than a "pulsation of divine life" (*ein Pulsschlag des göttlichen Lebens*). He must preserve a "being himself," some personal position of contrast, a separate ego for which dissolving into this divine universal-being is an infinite task: being one with God is conditioned by being other than God. This persistence of the separate "I," what I should call being children of oneselves, rooted in one's own autonomy as in the foundations of one's own basic identity, is for Simmel the condition which guarantees truly human relations—not merely mechanical and bureaucratic relations, predictable and taken for granted, between subjects living in society, nor the "relations between individuals and the individual circles (*Kreisen*) of their social connections."[11] The individual is thus produced by society, but at the same time produces it.[12] As Horkheimer and Adorno maintained, but even before them, Herbert Spencer, today there is ever more society, masses of human beings hitherto excluded appear on the historical stage and ask to participate; but it is also true, said Simmel, that this social diffusion does not dissolve our personality completely, just as it is true that the interior and exterior elements between individual and society are not determinations which exist simplistically one beside another, according to a model of discreet neighborliness. Rather, one must identify specifically the whole unitary position of the subject living in society. The presentation which sees in the individual a partially social and partly individual being is thus mechanical.

The problem posed by the individual in the modern world is that on the contrary he expresses indissolubly the synthesis and the contemporaneousness, existential and socially crystallized in the role, of the two determinations.

SOCIETY AS A STRUCTURE OF UNEQUAL ELEMENTS

The corollary of this conception is that "society is a construct of unequal elements." But democracy? Socialism? Simmel's response is very clear. Even where democratic or socialist tendencies plan and partly achieve an "equality," we are only ever dealing with an "equal valuation of persons" (*Gleichwertigkeit der Personen*), of productions and positions, while equality of men and women according to their natural qualities, according to the contents of their life and fortunes, cannot even be proposed as an object of discussion. Equal valuation of persons foreshadows their interchangeability, that is, the arrival of malleable man, like a machine part, in a social situation wherein the purely personal, internally productive, element, the impulses and reflexes of the real "I" (*die Impulse und Reflexe des eigentlichen Ichs*)[13] are perceived and considered as disturbing factors for the general plan. In other words, the life of society develops as though everything were already preordered because of the position each element occupies within the whole. The section with which Herbert Marcuse begins *One-Dimensional Man* comes to mind: "A comfortable, smooth, reasonable, democratic unfreedom prevails in advanced industrial civilization, a token of technical progress. Indeed, what could be more rational than the suppression of individuality in the mechanization of socially necessary but painful performances; the concentration of individual enterprises in more effective, more productive corporations; the regulation of free competition among unequally equipped subjects; the curtailment of prerogatives and national sovereignties which impede the international organization of resources. [*sic*] That this technological order also involves a political and intellectual coordination may be a regrettable and yet promising development."[14]

THE CATEGORY OF PROFESSION

The conceptual and organizational instrument whereby this process of absolute socialization is effected, and which leads to one-dimensional man through the cancellation of individual characteristics, is for Simmel the category of *profession*. In this regard too, Simmel's problematic sensitivity is striking. What was to appear in Marcuse as a kind of reductio ad absurdum is presented here in a much more nuanced way. It is indeed true, he remarked, that the ancient world did not know the concept of profession as the differentiation of persons and of society joined on the basis of the principle of the division of labor. However, the basis of the concept of profession, or that socially effective action is the unitary expression of internal qualification, was certainly known to the ancient world, which knew that for there to be a vocation in the full sense, that of *Beruf*, which is profession and at the same time a religious-spiritual "calling," it is necessary for there to be considerable harmony between society on the one hand and individual impulses and attitudes on the other. Naturally, the form of society must not be confused with the motivation, or, as Weber was to say, the social action, of individuals. Society as such can be studied as a totality of pure forms, and it is in this study, according to Simmel, that the object and justification of sociology lie. He said: "The causal connection which links every social element to the being and doing of every other element, thus forming the external network of society, is transformed into a teleological one as soon as it (the connection) is analyzed by its individual supports, its producers, who see themselves as individuality, and whose conduct (*Verhalten*) grows as a personality meaningful and existing in itself."[15] Possibly in no other work does Simmel more brilliantly show the functional needs of society and "consciousness"—in Marxist terms the "false consciousness" of the individual subjects—than in *The Philosophy of Money*, presented not only in psychologizing terms, but also as regards institutional groupings which are decisive for a given society. The rhythms of evolution vary at times so as to deepen the contrasts. "To this schema belong the cases which have been summed up in the fact that the relations of production, after prevailing in a given epoch, are exceeded by the forces of production which they developed, so that the former no longer allow the latter adequate expression and use. . . . The necessary transformation of the forms occurs only when the determining motives have been accumulated in large quantities, to the point where the material organization of production remains behind with respect to the development of individual economic energies. Many motives in the feminist movement come into this schema. The progress of modern industrial technique have transferred many domestic activities formerly in the province of women, out of the house, where objects can be made more cheaply. Thus now for many women of the bourgeois class, the active content of life has been taken away without other activities and trades being introduced equally rapidly in their place; the multiple 'dissatisfaction' of modern women, the inability to use their strength, which, rebounding on themselves, cause every possible disturbance or damage—their partly healthy, partly sick search for affirmation outside the house—all this is the result of the fact that technique in its objectivity has made its own advance, one more rapid than the possibilities of development of persons."[16]

The above is just one example Simmel's subtle and brilliant insights into the forms and content of social life. In the real sense the sociological category is for him only form. For this reason, "formal sociology"—in Simmel's sense—is essentially concerned with relationships within human groups based on the assumption that despite their extraordinary variety and the changes in historical existence, they demonstrate a formal equality and are thus independent of their content. If, however, the object of sociological knowledge is given by the forms as abstracted from their content, this does not mean that social forms can be identified with "social formations" or "modes of behavior." In reality, "social forms" in his view can only be found where human beings enter into relation with one another, and exercise mutual influence.

NOTES

1. The term is appropriately used by Kurt H. Wolff in his preface to the volume he edited, *Essays on Sociology, Philosophy and Aesthetics*, New York: Harper and Row, 1965.

2. Cf. G. Simmel, *Soziologie: Üntersuchungen über die Formen der Vergellschaftung*, Leipzig: Duncker & Humbolt, 1908, p. 27.

3. Simmel, *Soziologie*, p. 28.

4. Simmel, *Soziologie*, p. 32.

5. Simmel, *Soziologie*, p. 33: "Um den Menschen zu Erkennen, sehen wir ihn nicht nach seiner reinen Individualität, sondern getragen erhoben oder auch erniedight durch den algemeinen Typus, unter den wir ihn rechnen."

6. Simmel, *Soziologie*, p. 34.

7. Simmel, *Soziologie*, p. 35.

8. Simmel, *Soziologie*, p. 35: "Jedes Element einer Gruppe nicht nur Gesellschaftsteil, sondern ausserdem noch etwas ist."

9. Simmel, *Soziologie*, p. 37.

10. Simmel, *Soziologie*, p. 38: ." . . die individuelle Seele nie innerhalb einer Verbindung stehen kann, ausserhalb deren sie nicht zugleich steht, . . . sie in keiner Ordnung eingestehlt ist, ohne sich zugleich ihr gegenuber zu finden."

11. Simmel, *Soziologie*, p. 39.

12. This contradiction, which in existential terms may arrive at an awareness accompanied by painful schizoid ambivalence, especially in modern rationalized society, has not always been grasped by contemporary sociologists, for whom, however, the "process of production" of society through the communicative relationship among its inhabitants has not been overlooked (cf., for example, the importance of *conversation* for Peter L. Berger, under the influence of A. Schutz, or the

débats for A. Touraine in *Production de la société*. They lack the sense of the contradictory dualism between the individual *in himself* and the *social* individual).

13. Simmel, *Soziologie*, p. 43.

14. Cf. H. Marcuse, *One-Dimensional Man*, Boston: Beacon Press, 1964, p. 1.

15. Simmel, *Soziologie*, p. 45.

16. See G. Simmel, *Philosophie des Geldes*, Leipzig, 1990; cited from my translation in *La Sociologia*, Milano: Garzanti, 1974, pp. 142–43. (English tran: *The Philosophy of Money*, trans. by T. Bottomore & D. Frisby, London: Routledge & Kegan Paul, 1978). It scarcely needs mentioning that Simmel's elaborations and research regarding the foreigner, fashion, adventure, the social function of conflict, and so on provide the contemporary reader with information and material for reflection as broad as they are qualitatively rich.

8

✛

Gabriel Tarde: Society as Mimetic Process

THE RECOVERY OF THE SUBINSTITUTIONAL SPHERE

Consider the position of thinkers and writers whose fate it is to be overshadowed if not totally blotted out by the good fortune of a great contemporary. This happened to Schopenhauer vis-à-vis Hegel. Schopenhauer's cutting observation in his *Parerga und Paralipomena* that Hegel's reputation was only the echo of the booming void in the mind of his audience, who were, moreover, very numerous, was for many years of little comfort to the solitary author of *The World as Will and Representation*. The same relationship of rivalry and, at the same time, resentment may be said to have been established between Gabriel Tarde and Émile Durkheim. In any reading, Durkheim must be acknowledged as a master, the root and source of an influence which has profoundly marked the direction of French sociology and even today can inspire stimulating and "current" interpretations. Tarde, on the other hand, though crowning his career with the Chair of Philosophy at the Collège de France, could never assemble a group of dedicated disciples, nor does his thought demonstrate the compelling logical character and sober, inner coherence of Durkheim's theoretical construct.

A contemporary of Herbert Spencer and Giosué Carducci, educated in the years in which Émile Zola and Vilfredo Pareto came to maturity, Tarde, like Durkheim and Comte, had, moreover—this seems a characteristic of many sociologists—a clearly provincial origin. However, it was accompanied by a manner of thought in which one can easily identify heterogeneous, if not contradictory, elements. First of all, there is a general attitude or orientation, thoroughly scientistic, which is expressed in an unshaken faith in the "magnificent and progressive destinies" of humanity. This basic optimism does not seem to have been seriously injured by the grave crisis which was to sweep away the Second Empire with the defeat at Sedan; and Tarde also emerges essentially unharmed by the moral discomfort and political problems of the Third Republic which, at the same time, fatally distressed Émile Durkheim's moralistic temperament. Second, alongside this lay-religion of progress, which was an important ingredient of the "spirit of the time," was a basic "humanism," tied, however, to faith in social statistics. This faith was so deeply rooted and unreserved as to make Tarde omit even the qualitative differences between the human world and the world of nature in a perspective of universal evolutionary progress, popularized at the time by Herbert Spencer, but also sufficient to allow one to see Tarde as one of the pioneers of mathematical methods and techniques of empirical research applied to the social sciences. With this, however, one should not think that one has confronted a thought even touched by a certain indulgence toward deterministic, materialistic, "reistic" conceptions, to some extent and in some way, limiting human behavior. In reality, and somewhat contradictorily, for Tarde the liberation of humankind is to be sought in the discovery of the individual and in the possibility of scientific and mathematical—or sociographic and statistical—analysis of individual behavior.

The fruits of this formulation were not to be long awaited. Tarde wrote in the conclusion of his basic work *Les lois de l'imitation* (*The Laws of Imitation*), "Now there will open up the most beautiful bloom of social life, aesthetic life, which, as an exception so rare and still so incomplete among us, will become general by fulfilling itself. Social life, with its complicated mechanisms of subduing functions, of monotonous repetitions, will finally appear as what it is: as the organic life of which it is the result and the complement. This is a long, dark and tortuous passage from elementary diversity to personal physiognomy."[1]

It is hard to conceive of anything further from Durkheim's thought, his insistence on the resilience of institutions, and his concept of anomie, than this scientific individualism which in some passages does not seem far from taking on a basic note of Leibnitzian optimism. It has been observed that the distinction between Tarde and Durkheim should not be sought in individualism so much as in the fact that as a good Enlightenment figure Tarde believes the theme of institutions to be secondary, while this is basic for Durkheim.[2] I do not find acceptable this method of presenting the problem of the relations between Tarde and Durkheim. The relative devaluation of the institutional moment on Tarde's part, what necessarily makes him, as has been said, a pioneer in research on social psychology and market analysis, by definition indifferent to the historical context and the specific political-institutional context (up to the contemporary research of Paul F. Lazarsfeld), must in fact be linked to the strictly individualistic formulation of Tarde.

According to this, the individual is both starting point and ultimate finishing point of human affairs. There is more. The individual is also essentially a self-sufficient reality, endowed with powers of management, adaptation, and opposition which are relatively adequate. Like certain insects, equipped by nature with a kind of internal radar, the human individual too, according to Tarde, is naturally capable of orienting himself or herself toward the social moment, thanks to a basic mimetic impulse which guarantees his or her sense of direction both at the individual level and the social-institutional one. Tarde has faith in the individual, and in this may be rightly identified as an Enlightenment figure in the classic sense of the term. However, it is precisely this faith which is totally lacking or is much diminished in great social thinkers who are his contemporaries, such as Durkheim or Freud. For Durkheim, as moreover for the Freud of the "reality principle" and the "pleasure principle," the individual is a danger; he has an explosive potential which can put at risk the social order; he has to be contained and corrected in his desires; he needs a "superego" or a "collective consciousness" which regulates and directs him. For Durkheim, anomie is the result of a discrepancy between the excessive aspirations of the individual and the effective possibility of satisfying them on the part of social institutions.

The long polemic which for years set Durkheim against Tarde certainly brought out the serious inaccuracies with which the relationship between sociology and psychology were understood.[3]

Especially in *Suicide*, Durkheim insisted on the externality and transcendance of the collective consciousness as regards individual consciousness. He saw in collective consciousness the source of action and basic moral values. However, as he enunciated its aprioristic nature as regards individual consciousness, he was therefore forced to see in it as well the source of every manifestation of individual consciousness, even negative ones, such as, for example, suicide. The way out of the contradiction can only be found in the direction pointed out by Parsons, whose analysis in this respect seems convincing that the social and psychopathological explanations of suicide are not antithetical but complementary.[4] For this reason, the two great adversaries fall into the same uncertainty and commit the same error. They ignore the fact that "the essential phenomenon of collective psychology is the reciprocal immanence and dialectic between collective consciousness and individual consciousness."[5]

A "LEVELED OUT" INDIVIDUALISM

Gabriel Tarde is thus an individualist sociologist. In this sociophilosophi-
cal conception, we see reflected precisely his social position and his theoretical premises: that is to say, his position in the class structure of French
society at the time (middle bourgeois employees with provincial agrarian
roots: a deep need for individual recognition in terms of status and sub-
sequent professional prestige, combined with great insecurity and a basic
gregariousness); at the same time, his ideological orientation, or principles of personal preference, which under analysis appear vaguely humanitarian and, at the most, utopian. However, what type of individualism are we dealing with?

In order to reply fully to this question, one must examine Tarde's
thought as expressed in *The Laws of Imitation* and *Les lois sociales* (*Social
Laws*), and retrace the fairly complex and not always linear parabola behind the agile elegance of his writing. The basic principle, which is at the
same time the explanatory and interpretative key to historical experience
and social relations, lies in his view of imitation or, more precisely, in the
double principle of invention and imitation variously combined. This
double principle in reality fits perfectly and to Tarde explains not only the
human world, but also the natural one, from the mineral to the vegetable
and the animal, to use Spencer's terminology.

Faced with this statement, and similar general statements of nineteenth-
century sociology, which are too prone to explain social and natural facts
from a single factor, or a universal principle, based on a somewhat crude
monocausality (not to say an ingenuous one), a certain amazement is permissible. Can one really reduce social and cosmic life to a reiterative
process, a repetitive formula? Tarde was aware of the seeming banality of
"universal repetition," with which he opens his basic work. But his certainty is not even minimally scratched by this. "Socially, everything con-
sists of inventions and imitations, and in the former there are the rivers of
which the latter are the mountains: there is nothing less subtle, certainly,
than this view; but by following it boldly, without reservations, by explaining it from the smallest detail to the fullest totality of facts, we shall
perhaps see how suitable it is to bring out everything which is pictur-
esque and at the same time all the simplicity, in history, to reveal perspectives bizarre as rocky landscape or regular as the pathways in a
park."[6]

One might say that Tarde, from these first remarks, is fully aware of the
accusations of idealism and especially of psychologism which were to
rain down upon him. He does not seem excessively worried about this.
He confines himself to noting that he means "to explain history through

the ideas of its actors and not those of the historian." The polemic against historians, explicit or implicit, is a constant in Tarde's work. His normal target is the intuitive or artistic historian, who imposes his ideas, intuitions, or preferences on the protagonists of the historical process itself, thus restricting its space to the great heroes and neglecting as irrelevant the whole ensemble of social relations which, rather, are the flesh—as it were—of historical development. Tarde's tone, if not his words, makes one think of what Paul Veyne wrote recently: "Sociology is a history unaware of itself."[7] It should be enough to reverse the terms. History is a sociology forgetful of itself, so distracted as to become crudely mutilated in its basic processes of social aggregation: that is, the innovation and imitation which are its permanent warp and woof.

However, it is not only history which must be incorporated or restored to sociology. Tarde notes "from this point of view, one sees the object of social science presenting a noteworthy analogy with other fields of general science and returning, as it were, to incorporate itself in the rest of the universe in whose bosom it had the appearance of being an extraneous body."[8] This reference is extraordinary. In German historicist culture the individualist outlook, as again with Max Weber, was in itself sufficient to support a distinction, if not a real break, between sciences of nature and sciences of the spirit of culture.

Here, exactly, the opposite occurs. The individual, viewed atomistically, becomes the moment, the unit, the item of a sequence or arithmetically expressable series, and in any case one perfectly manipulable according to the rules and logic of mathematical language. Hence, not only is the individual not an *arcanum*, something unique, irreducible, and unrepeatable, but on the contrary he emerges as the basic unit of scientific measurement which we require. He is the hinge of our knowledge and of exact measurements, the essential term. One understands how Tarde might thus represent the link between Cournot and Lazarsfeld. "Every time that *to produce* does not mean *reproduce oneself*, for us all becomes shadowy."[9] For Tarde, the contrast between world of nature and historical world has no meaning: "the social being as such is essentially an imitator . . . imitation in society plays a role analogous to that of heredity in organisms or the wave in brute forces."[10]

Tarde's reasoning is clear. Science is the science of uniformity and regularity, expressed in "laws." In order to guarantee the possibility of a social science, one must thus determine a principle of regularity for the historic or social world as well. This principle exists and is the principle of imitation. Even the simplest introspective examination suffices to provide us with this certainty: "Then one would realize that the confused illogic of the facts of history, all decomposable into different currents of examples, of which they are the meeting- point (itself destined to be more or less exactly copied), is no proof against the basic regularity of the social world and against the possibility of a social science. One would really realize that this science exists, dispersed, in the small experience of each one of us, and that one has to recompose its fragments."[11]

According to Tarde, social science must thus "exclusively concern multiple similar facts." According to Tarde's definition, not science but social philosophy should concern itself with the other facts, that is, the extraordinary "new and dissimilar" facts. Social science should look to concerning itself with social uniformities, just as the sciences of nature are concerned with classifying natural phenomena which have one or more characteristics in common. Thus, he concludes, to be involved in social science means to be involved in imitation and its laws.

At this point of the development of Tarde's thought, there is an incredible parallel which opens up between his theoretical apparatus and that of Spencer. As for Spencer the principle of universal evolution was the basis of the explanatory criterion and, in a cosmic sense, the general law, so for Tarde the principle of imitation concerns "the chemical, physical, and astronomical world . . . which has as its sole explanation and possible cause periodic and mainly oscillatory movements." Second, it also concerns the living world (hereditary transmission, analogy, and homology of every type in physiology and anatomy). Finally, it explains all similarities of social origin which are "the direct or indirect product of imitation in all its forms—imitation-habit or imitation-fashion, imitation-sympathy or imitation-obedience, imitation-instruction or imitation-education, ingenuous imitation or premeditated imitation."[12]

Tarde's individualism does not thus exclude, but rather is based on leveling. Contrary to Spencer's, it is an atomistic and mechanistic individualism. One would be tempted to dismiss it as a new, little revisited version of the *homme-machine* of De La Mettrie, were it not accompanied by certain striking intuitions. "Doesn't one see from its beginnings, how this prodigious levelling might make possible the birth and development of statistics and what has been rightly called *social physics*, political economy? Without fashion and habit, there would be no social quantity."[13] Moreover, Tarde establishes the concept of prediction in the field of the social sciences as "a conditioned prediction." He notes: "it is said that without the ability to foresee, there is no science. Let us correct this: yes, without the ability of *conditioned* prediction. . . . The physicist can say that this shot fired at this moment will be heard in a certain number of seconds at a certain distance, so long as nothing interrupts the noise of its trajectory. . . . It is precisely in this way that the sociologist deserves the name of scientist in the real sense. Given that today there are such centers of diffusion of imitation which tend to move forward separately or jointly at approximate speeds, he is capable of predicting what will be the social state within ten or twenty years, *on the condition that any political reform or revolution does not interrupt this expansion and that no rival centers arise.*"[14] That is, the sociologist can explain history and advance historical predictions as well, provided history denies itself, refuses to develop, and ends in a kind of still-life. However, these are the same requirements recently expressed by Paul Lazarsfeld. While measuring exactly, mathematically, human behavior, he does not refrain from suppressing the qualities which make them human, mobile, meaningful, unpredictable (or, more precisely, predictable only *conditionally*).

One might say that Tarde is aware of this difficulty. He had hardly finished describing the three forms of Repetition, in fact too schematically and dogmatically (undulation, oscillation or generation, imitation) not to recall, by analogy, Auguste Comte's law of the three states, which poses the problem of how to explain the object of imitation, that is, invention. How can the cycle of imitative and repetitive routine be interrupted? How can invention be explained?

Once the leveling of the individual has been accepted, the problem becomes difficult for Tarde, the more so that he cannot use the purely mechanical resources of the system nor invoke ideological factors (as a "teleological thrust") nor, ultimately, could he refer to the material interests which in this regard he tended to underrate. The path of "instincts," generally open to more or less orthodox Spencerians, especially of a Darwinian persuasion, is closed to him and in this sense Tarde's position is certainly more difficult than that of Thorstein Veblen and his "instinct of workmanship," connected with the socioanthropological theory of man as "free agent," also as *homo fuber*, not so much "creator" as "transformer of the environment," and in this sense a toolmaker, artisan.

Tarde's explanation looks like a shortcut, and one of the less convincing ones: that is, a mechanistic shortcut expressed in two vaguely psychological terms as to avoid being called psychologistic. "On the one hand one must not lose sight of the fact that the need of inventing and discovering develops—like every other need—by satisfying oneself. On the other, that every invention may be reduced to the happy intersection of one intelligent mind, of one current of imitation, with another current of imitation which reinforces it in the present with an intense external perception which makes a received idea emerge in an unforeseen light, . . . psychological elements formed under the influence of the sample."[15] In other words, invention, too, in reality is a kind of imitation: "Everything which in the phenomena of society is social and not vital or physical, both in its analogies and its differences, is caused by imitation."[16]

What, then, is a society? Tarde replies, "imitation."[17] But what is imitation? Tarde no longer replies directly. He defers to the psychologist. Society becomes the group: "a collection of beings in that they are imitating each other and in that, without actually imitating each other, they resemble each other, since their common traits are old copies of the same model."[18]

SOCIETY AS MIMETIC PROCESS
AND THE FUNCTION OF THE SMALL GROUP

The psychologist is not enough. One needs also the services of the neurologist. The macrosociological framework of society as a complex of more or less formally and rigidly codified structures becomes increasingly distant, is clouded over, and finally sinks. Real reality for Tarde is provided by the mimetic flows at the interindividual and intraindividual level: "The essential social fact, as I see it, to be fully understood, demands the knowledge of infinitely delicate cerebral facts. . . . Sociology which is apparently most clear, even that which appears on the surface sinks its roots into psychology, into the most intimate and obscure physiology. *Society is imitation, and imitation is a kind of sleep-walking*. . . . We have seen that in sleepwalkers or quasi-sleepwalkers memory is very vivid as to habit (muscular memory, as we stated earlier), while credulity and docility are prepared to the utmost. In other words, in them *imitation of themselves by themselves* . . . is as noteworthy as the imitation of others."[19]

It is difficult to deny the current significance of these remarks and simply reject them together with the whole mechanistic apparatus in which they seem to be inserted. This would be theoretically improper and morally ungenerous. Tarde's comments—language and naturalistic analogies aside—maintain high suggestibility and seem to foretell directly theoretical and research work which has only recently been fully developed.

Tarde rejected the attempt of John Stuart Mill to place the foundation of sociology on the supposed psychological laws of human nature, just as he would probably have rejected "the psychology of associated minds" set out brilliantly by Carlo Cattaneo. Tarde is also harshly critical of Herbert Spencer, who saw society as a social organism in the true biological sense, with all the limits of a homostatic model applied to the historical world (limits which were to return in an accentuated form in the various versions of contemporary structural functionalism). As well, he criticizes Gustave Le Bon, who had laid out a "psychology of crowds" as though the crowd was an entity provided with its own real autonomy, independently of the individuals who are the concrete elements which make it up.

For Tarde, too, society is a collective reality, but it must not be hypostasized. It does not exist outside the individuals who make it up. It is not permissible to speak of an abstract "collective consciousness" or "human nature" or "crowd psychology," but only of "laws" drawn from the analysis of the relationships which occur between one individual and another. These relationships are governed by imitation. Imitation generates uniformities, fashions, customs, language, and religions. In particular, imitation creates habit, and this gives rise to the characteristic automatism of individual behavior, which is the essence of everyday life and which is, on the other hand, typical of every mimetic impulse at the semiconscious level. Here, Tarde's remarks bring to mind Simmel's research and the "relational sociology" of Leopold von Wiese, the "mental construction of the everyday world" of Schutz, the "generalized other" of G. H. Mead, Herbert Blumer's "symbolic interactionism," and the analyses of current ethnomethodologists.

However, possibly the strongest and best theoretically based referent, in the sense of a real continuity or at least a critical rerun, is that which exists between Tarde's thought and the attempts to make a theoretical foundation for empirical social research by Paul F. Lazarsfeld. The latter complains initially of what Tarde believes impossible: a measurement of attitudes insofar as "psychological statistics which might illustrate changes in specific individuals"[20] are lacking. Elsewhere, however, he acknowledges that "public opinion stopped being a discourse of general speculation and became the object of specific and particular monographs. Among these there was a series of papers by Gabriel Tarde. . . . In one of these articles, Tarde dealt with the effect that the influences on the external world, such as newspapers, had in the process of forming opinions. However, the analysis that he regarded as basic was contained in his *La Conversation*.[21] He was convinced that opinions were in fact formed through the interchange of comments and observations which took place day by day among individuals. His ideas are very close to our concept of the process of fulfilment. Precisely through the simple process which exists in speaking to another, the vague attitudes which an individual has gradually crystallize into attitudes, actions and specific positions. He intuited that an accurate empirical study of conversations was basic for society, and he proposed a large number of hypotheses of this type. Who is speaking, to whom, about what and how much does he say. All this in terms of the social characteristics of the interlocutors and changes in the historical environment."[22] Lazarsfeld thus sees in Tarde a precursor of his theory concerning "personal influence."[23] This theory had, and still has, a great influence among researchers and interpreters of mass communications and their media, the messages they send out and their meaning—clearly massified—for the members of modern mass society. It played a role of reassurance. From Marshall McLuhan to Roman Gubern, there was and is the fear for the future of today's individuals' rationality, that is, their ability to keep their head and not be preyed upon by the uninterrupted flow of communications and messages. The "message is the massage": the "means is the content," McLuhan warned paradoxically, but up to a point. Lazarsfeld had, for a while, pressed forward.

It was wrong to think on the one hand that there was a means of mass communication, solitary, mysterious, and omnipotent, and on the other the disconnected, amorphous essentially passive "mass." In reality, Lazarsfeld argues, between the "means" and the "mass," there is the small group with its complex network of channels of communication, its structures of meaning and language, and with the fluid, unpredictable interpersonal relationships—rich and dense though they are—which characterize them. In other words, there is a "conversation," which Tarde had already spoken of and written about seventy years earlier. Analogously, but possibly not irrelevantly, Lazarsfeld and Katz, in proposing their "rediscovery" of the "small group," repeat on a larger scale the conceptual research which, still in the United States, Elton G. Mayo carried out, with his studies on the "human problems in industry," in turn referring back to Durkheim's concept of anomie and in the figure of the new "demiurgic administrator"—at once technician and politician—taking on again the elitist proposals of Mosca and Pareto.

With the rediscovery of the small group, seen as the decisive and nodal point for the structuring and orientation of public opinion, Lazarsfeld and his associates undoubtedly satisfied and performed a reassuring function. The theme of the research should no longer be sought in mass communications in themselves, in those who control them and in the quality of the messages they transmit, nor should mass society be investigated as such. Rather, one should devise research techniques suitable for the study of the small group—that is, the critical filter of messages diffused by the media. Hence there arises, in terms of theory and research, the need of closely linking the study of the informal group with the study of the effects of mass communications. And so arises the hypothesis of the *two-step flow of communication* and the need of providing the technical apparatus capable of understanding and explaining its substance and effects. If in fact the primary group essentially has a basic role in conditioning the acceptance or refusal of the messages transmitted by the mass media, then we are concerned with seeing what parameters the selection of the content of the messages themselves are concerned with, on whose part, and for what ends.

Critical demands of the same type, however, concern mass society itself and its established characteristics. Tarde stresses conversation, messages exchanged between one individual and another. Peter Berger does not speak much differently about the sociologist and phenomenologist Alfred Schutz. However, in this respect Tarde is totally of the nineteenth century, that is, an age in which rationality had not yet abandoned the individual to become an attribute of the great bureaucratic and personal organizations, nor had society completely abandoned the great traditions and "the authority of the eternal yesterday" to become a "mass scientific society." Science for today's type of society has a certain price. Not so much because we are dealing with civilization of the image, of a world of idols, of "things to see," rather than about issues to be debated.

There is no doubt that contemporary science, which has now become a directly productive force, which transcends traditional technology as applied science gives priority to visual immediacy at the total loss of smell, taste, and hearing. The noise of traffic and of certain pop music conspire together to create a generation of the deaf, while the current fashion of deodorants removes distasteful pungent odors. Modern science demands an ascetic environment. The object is no longer attained, nor directly manipulated. It is "read" by way of the written record or what is visibly ascertainable through instruments. Experience is always more looked at than lived through. It tends to be an ambiguous, ultimately contradictory, experience: it participates but is distanced. It is and is not. More than a civilization of the image, one should thus speak of a society of voyeurs. People who, rather than performing as principals, confine themselves to looking. Instead of trying things out as actors, they confine themselves to sitting in the audience.

It is normal that in such a society a flood of "iconic" messages develops along with the growth of a mass culture on the ruins of the great peasant traditions which are swept away or perverted by the process of industrialization. There also arise numerous languages, codes, means of information, and flows of communication. Their limit, to which Tarde and also Lazarsfeld do not appear to pay the necessary attention, was very well established by Roman Gubern. "The greatness and poverty of messages . . . lies in the fact that like dreams, they cannot aspire wholly to replace personal and direct experience of life and history, which shapes the awareness of citizens and which ultimately explains what, in reality, they are. Any changes in decisive factors carried out in their environment and their global context, would be capable of causing a profound change in their convictions and their most important and basic attitudes."[24]

INDIVIDUALISM DESTINED TO RISE AGAIN AFTER SOCIALISM

We have thus returned to the basic contradiction, that which underlies the brilliant, individualist-atomistic construct of Tarde, and which at the same time unveils Lazarsfeld's apologetic intent. The image, the iconic message, while filtered through the small group placed between the media and the mass, at the moment in which it provides the greatest profit with the minimal expense, in fact robs us of a knowledge and a real human participation: that is, one which is unpredictable and dramatic. Life touches us but through a third party. It is a reflected life which does not live, it is an *imitated life*, the shadow of a shadow. Ultimately, it is a secondhand life. The spectator enjoys a passive participation, a vicarious enjoyment. This is the forechamber of mental passivity and political inertia: the necessary premise to a manipulation which in the case of technically advanced societies, sufficiently depersonalized and dynamic, becomes a kind of internal colonization and proletarianization of the soul—or, the resolution and adoption of the individual in the formula "production and consumption." No one lives. One is impersonally lived. From the starting point and the point of arrival, the individual is simply weakened, flattened, and homogenized to the point of dissolution.

This critique, which was in particular brought to its extreme conclusion by Adorno and Horkheimer, as regards the contradictions of late capitalism, should not therefore be included in an apocalyptic perspective or one of romantic catastrophe. We know that the message is variously filtered and does not pass from the screen to the individual spectator. It is mediated and decomposed and reconstituted by the primary group to which the individual belongs. However, the problem remains open. What happens when the filter of the "public," understood as the totality of small primary groups, relatively autonomous as regards the outside world, is as such destroyed? When the small primary group is dissolved or has lost its traditional importance as "street corner society"? When, in other words, have we entered into a full, mass industrial society? Then, it is no longer necessary to propose manipulation as an objective to be attained. To attain the maximum mystifying effect, it is enough that the mass media should say, simply and purely, everything, according to a positivist criterion of naturalistic objectivity: that is, putting on the same level all information as items of the same news report, offered to isolated, fragmented, and atomized individuals, thus unable to resist its pressure.

That we are dealing with a real problem is now tranquilly admitted by everyone. Faced with the danger of parasitism and thereafter mass mystification determined by a center which decides arbitrarily and a fragmented periphery incapable of making meaningful reactions, it has been proposed to overturn the relationship between center and periphery, either by cable TV or other technical means. However, even staying on the technical level, it is doubtful that the question can be resolved. In fact, the question is one of power, that is, a political one. The media are instruments of power: Whose power? For what? They reemerge from the shadow where the material interests of life discretely weave their webs, together with their stubborn physiological tendency to transform public need into private choice, into power as an exclusive and discretional fief, power as service and rational function.

Brilliant analyses like Tarde's, or technically refined ones, like those of Lazarfeld, do not manage to scratch the surface, nor even to glimpse it. We may admire their elegance, but we cannot be silent about their limits.

Lazarfeld is not wholly unaware of these when he asks: "What aspects of popular sentiments are meaningful for the analysis of social events?"[25] He correctly recalls that Tarde distinguishes between "tradition," "opinion" and "fashion," whereas Ferdinand Toennies had recourse to two basic conceptual categories, "community" (*Gemeinschaft*) and "society" (*Gesellschaft*). Finally, he agrees with the vague concept that historians term "climate of opinion."

Here too, there is still a pressing question: can one still speak of "climate of opinion" when it is no longer permissible to speak of "opinion"? In fact, after C. Wright Mills and others in the United States, as well as in Europe, it is difficult to speak of "public opinion" as one could speak of it in the nineteenth century, when by saying "society" one really meant a restricted one dominated by specific elite values (in the sense of the expression "to enter society"). Strictly speaking, one must agree that mass society has neither a public in the real sense, nor a public opinion, relatively autonomous as regards the major sources of mass information.

It may be that Shils is right, as against the critical reservations of the Frankfurt School, and that mass society is really a society based on consensus, on the transcendence of the rupture between masses and elites, and the increasingly capillary diffusion of moral egalitarianism. However, if this is the case, one must recognize, together with Tocqueville, and David Riesman, the theoretician of "other-directedness," it was Tarde who demonstrated how the mechanism functions, explaining how egalitarianism and consensus in mass society are more the result of a conformist herd-instinct linked to repetition and reiteration than the conquest of a qualitatively higher and politically more logical and rich life.[26]

Here and there in Tarde's work one sees disturbing questions and predictions in this regard: "The monotonous play of generations without the individual variations of living human beings, the monotonous play of the rippling of the ether, molecular or stellar, with no kind of diversity,—meteorological, astronomical, geographical, chemical: the monotonous play of imitation, even in the most noble and rational civilizations, without aesthetic originality, without the historical novelties in every moment and every place—of what use would all this be?"[27] Against these same logical consequences of this theoretical system, Tarde ends his research with a passionate anthem for the individual with a note which recalls in its emotional accents and aesthetic tendency, Oscar Wilde's famous pamphlet *The Soul of Man Under Socialism*. Tarde states: "Despite the socialist flood

which is being prepared, individualistic liberalism cannot die and ultimately will be reborn with greater semblances."[28]

It is not established that in this prophesy, or in other, similar predictions, the reason for the lasting interest in Tarde's work should be sought. The importance of Tarde's individualistic outlook does not lie in reasons of a contingent political order to which it may seem to be connected, but rather in the recognition it postulates of the decisive character of nonformally codifiable behavior at the subinstitutional level. From this behavior, its form and "style," much more than from formal juridical definitions, or at least to the same extent, there derives the quality of social life in a specific historical epoch.

NOTES

1. G. Tarde, *Les lois de l'imitation*, Paris: F. Alcan, 1904; cited from the Italian tran.: *La legge dell'imitazione*, in *Opere*, ed. F. Ferrarotti, Torino: UTET, 1975, pp. 411–12.

2. Cf. Friedrich Jonas, *Geschichte der Soziologie*, Hamburg: Rowohlt, 1968; cited from the Italian tran.: *Storia della sociologia*, trans. by Anna Maria Pozzan et al., Bari: Laterza, 1970, p. 383.

3. See my *Trattato di sociologia*, Torino: UTET, 1968, pp. 134ff.

4. Cf. T. Parsons, *The Structure of Social Action*, 2 vols., New York: Free Press, 1968: cited from the Italian trans.: *La struttura del'azione sociale*, Bologna: Il Mulino, 1962, p. 407.

5. Cf. Georges Gurvitch, *La vocation actuelle de la sociologie*, Paris: Presses Universitaires de France, 1950, p. 27.

6. Tarde, *Les lois de l'imitation*, p. 45.

7. Cf. Paul Veyne, *Writing History*, trans. by M. Moore-Rinvolucri, Middletown, Conn.: Wesleyan University Press, 1984.

8. Tarde, *Les lois de l'imitation*, p. 46.

9. Tarde, *Les lois de l'imitation*, p. 48 (my emphasis).

10. Tarde, *Les lois de l'imitation*, p. 53.

11. Tarde, *Les lois de l'imitation*, p. 54.

12. Tarde, *Les lois de l'imitation*, p. 56.

13. Tarde, *Les lois de l'imitation*, p. 58.

14. Tarde, *Les lois de l'imitation*, pp. 60–61 (my emphasis).

15. Tarde, *Les lois de l'imitation*, p. 86.

16. Tarde, *Les lois de l'imitation*, p. 952.

17. Tarde, *Les lois de l'imitation*, p. 117.

18. Tarde, *Les lois de l'imitation*, p. 111.

19. Tarde, *Les lois de l'imitation*, pp. 130–31.

20. See P. Lazarsfeld, "Notes on the History of Quantification in Sociology," in *Isis*, pt. 2, 1961, pp. 277–333; cited from the Italian trans. in Paul Lazarsfeld, *Metodologia e ricerca sociologica*, Bologna: Il Mulino, 1971, p. 101.

21. G. Tarde, *L'opinion et la foule*, Paris: F. Alcan, 1901, pp. 82–159.

22. Lazarsfeld, "Notes," p. 171.

23. Cf. Elihu Katz and Paul Lazarsfeld, *Personal Influence*, Glencoe, Ill.: Free Press, 1955; Italian trans.: *L'influenza personale nelle comunicazioni di massa*, Torino: Edizioni RAI, 1968.

24. See R. Gubern, *Mensajes ironicos en la cultura di massa*, Barcelona: Ed. Lumen, 1974, p. 377.

25. See Lazarsfeld, *Metodologia*, p. 899.

26. Cf. Edward A. Shils, "Mass Society and its Culture," in *Daedalus*, vol. 89, 1960, pp. 288–314; for the interpretations of mass society in Shils, Bramson, Kornhauser, and Bell, see C. Mannucci, *La società di massa*, Milano: Comunità, 1967.

27. Tarde, *Opere*, p. 553.

28. Tarde, *Opere*, p. 554.

9

+

Richard H. Tawney:
The Search for the
Doctrinal Foundation of
"Labor" Socialism

A PRAGMATIC SOCIALIST

Richard Henry Tawney lived from 1880 to 1962. He belonged to one of those illustrious families of high civil servants of the British crown, scattered in the Dominions throughout the world, for whose understanding William Henry Beveridge's *India Called Them* (1947) is basic (Beveridge was Tawney's brother-in-law). This was a social stratum of high prestige and extreme moral rectitude, real martyrs to good form, the backbone of the Administrative Class—almost a caste as regards customs and perpetuation. This was ensured by a system of cooperation fiercely defended against external pressures and interference in an almost absolute endogamic conditioning. The personalities, with very few exceptions (the Philby case, a sensation also because of its rarity, possibly also Bertrand Russell), which emerged from it seemed admirably functional for the social and political structure which expressed them by showing at once innovative spirit, but without revolutionary breaks, and respect for tradition and received values, literally "handed down" from the past, but without making a fetish of them. In this landscape Tawney, born in Calcutta, belonged to the innovative wing. This should not be surprising. In the English cultural and sociopolitical world, there are notable examples of the wealthy commercial bourgeoisie and the minor aristocracy who, in distinction to what generally happened in continental Europe, evolved and moved from right to left. Besides Sidney and Beatrice Webb, one might cite the case of Stafford Cripps and, for the most part, of the Fabians, whose socialism formed the mind and conscience of the labor movement, from John Strachey to G. D. H. Cole and Harold Laski.

In the path of this tradition, Tawney's curriculum vitae is indeed perfectly predictable. He was sent by his father, C. H. Tawney, rector of Presidency College, Calcutta, and his mother, Constance Catherine Fox, to England to finish his education—first to Rugby, then to Balliol College, Oxford, where he was elected Fellow from 1918 to 1924, becoming Honorary Fellow in 1938. He was appointed president of Morley College for working men and women from 1933 to 1937. In 1909 he married Annette J. Beveridge, who died in 1958 without issue.

However, Tawney's career was certainly not taken up wholly in the routine of teaching. Despite his anticonformist tendencies, at times in open and apparently radical conflict with the status quo, Tawney never felt (typically English also in this) any reluctance toward taking on responsibilities and consultancies, chairmanships of committees and management of institutions connected with the government of the day and the centers of economic and industrial power. It is virtually impossible to mention all his posts: among others, he was a member of the "Consultative Committee of the London Board of Education," the Coal Industry Commission, the Chain Trade Board, and the Cotton Trade Conciliation Committee. However, what is most striking is the open-mindedness, the clear pragmatic spirit with which the author of *The Acquisitive Society* accepted and performed, moreover outstandingly, tasks which to even a moderate socialist in continental Europe would certainly have appeared compromising. The war and the Churchill coalition government naturally explain many things. In 1942 he did in fact spend several months in Washington as counsellor on economic and social affairs at the British embassy, but it is also true that in 1913 and 1914 he was director of the Ratan Tate Foundation. Another curious fact: one who had devoted such a large part of his time and energy to the cause of the Labour Party was never an MP, never even sought a candidacy, nor really undertook direct political activity in the strictly party sense and at the party level. Rather, he always, at times with exceptional efficiency, exercised a notable political influence, indirectly—that is, a moral influence more of authoritativeness than authority, more of persuasion than power.

His work resounds with his direct participation in the management of public bodies and political and union life. When in 1949, as professor emeritus of economic history at the University of London, he retired to the peaceful greenery of Gloucestershire, he confined himself to writing occasional articles and essays for periodicals, many of which were later republished posthumously in *The Radical Tradition*. However, one can say that his main works span forty years or more, from the famous *The Agrarian Problem in the Sixteenth Century* (1912) to *Religion and the Rise of Capitalism* (1926) and *Equality* (1931). Essentially, we are dealing with works of economic sociology, but with a particular slant, a strong taste for the historical dimension of problems and underpinned by immense economic and also—very rare in sociologists—juridical erudition. This was a mixture not always capable of reaching a perfect degree of fusion and internal coherence, but almost always instructive and socially and politically committed.

RIGHTS AND FUNCTIONS

Perhaps one can understand today the reasons why Talcott Parsons, the most representative sociologist of his day, should have insisted on defining Tawney as "above all a moralist."[1] By tracing his biography, Parsons tried to dig deep to bring to light the directly and consciously religious roots of Tawney's radicalism. It is hard to deny this. Tawney was a devout Anglican, with pronounced tendencies toward High Church. Moreover, it should not be forgotten that he managed to live simultaneously, in Parsons's view, four careers (scholar, teacher, writer, and business man, or at least one devoted to organizational and political practice); he owed much to and had been deeply affected by the theological ideas and social convictions of Charles Gore, just as he had absorbed from his first years as a student the atmosphere of Rugby and Oxford as well as the close friendship of William Temple, future archbishop of Canterbury. So too one must bear in mind the experience of the young Tawney in the First World War when he volunteered for the Manchester Regiment and became and stayed a sergeant, though he could, with his political connections (espe cially through Arthur Henderson, minister of Labour), have opened the way to other, higher positions. However, still more important is the experience as union organizer for the miners in 1925, an initiative which led, along with many others, to the General Strike of 1926.

These facts and experience seem to escape Parsons's interpretation, perceptive though it is. Thus, when Parsons asserts, regarding Tawney's attitude to the society in which he lived, that he was "interested in it more as a moralist than as a scientist," one's disagreement can only be total. In Parsons's remarks there reappears the old-fashioned polemical opposition of "social critique" and "social science," or between politically oriented social research and distanced sociological analysis, presumed to be neutral. Those who hold this opposition subdivide scholars of social questions into two large categories, corresponding more or less to two psychological types: the tough-minded, given to consider facts and objective realities, without indulging in possibly brilliant but unverifiable thoughts; and the soft-minded, or sentimental, who, in their generous but incautious thirst to help humanity, systematically confuse the level of analytic ascertainment with that of therapeutic operation, giving rise to a confused situation in which neither science nor philanthropy is rescued.

This contrast is based on a sophistry. It presupposes that "facts speak for themselves, and that there is thus possible a sociological study of them which is absolutely neutral, without values, 'distanced.'" Anyone with direct experience of research knows instead that the facts do not speak for themselves, and that the only way to make them meaningful and interpretable lies in having available a theoretical-conceptual apparatus which is not and cannot be gratuitous, but more or less exactly corresponds to selective criteria connected with the problems, political preferences, and ideological tendencies of the researchers. The so-called neutrality of much sociological research is no more than the fragile screen through which, expressed in scientific jargon which is often more than necessarily obscure, the political and ideological choices—the "values"—of the researchers are smuggled in; researchers who on the contrary see themselves as "neutral" and "objective."

In Tawney's primary works there is no trace of this pompous "scientific neutrality." Besides the works of strictly historical reconstruction, take *The Acquisitive Society* (1921), *Religion and the Rise of Capitalism* (1926), or *Equality* (1931). In these, the rigorous analysis of the factual data of historical situations and juridical institutions is always accompanied by an attempt at interpretation so socially committed as to give rise, in some cases, to real perorations as, for example, one sees in the conclusions of works of social analysis from Shaw to Cole, Laski and lately Anthony Crosland.[2] But Tawney goes beyond them, and stands with full scientific authority and the originality of his problematic, as an interlocutor of the first rank alongside Max Weber, together with the dense crowd in which the names of Troeltsch, Brentano, Wunsch, Sombart, and so forth stand out—to arrive in our time at the undoubtedly brilliant if controversial one of Herbert Luthy.[3]

The principal concern of Tawney, as J. D. Chambers notes,[4] was the secularization of Christian values in the sixteenth and seventeenth centuries—the major secular event of Western civilization, and the basis of the setting-up of an "acquisitive society," which represents at the same time the end of the medieval attempt to moralize economic life. To Tawney, what was a weakness of nature to Adam Smith became a solid virtue.

On his part, Parsons observed that Weber and Tawney are more or less identified, but wrongly so, in spite of the important connection between the two. They share the accent placed on the importance of religion in this historical-social context. They also agree that there was a rupture in the Protestant movement from this point of view, in that, in its influence on economic development, the Lutheran branch (above all Luther himself) was virtually medieval, while the Calvinist branch, including Calvin, was much more "favorable" to the general dynamics of economic development. Even more so was later Protestantism.

However, the differences between the two are important. For Tawney, the influence of Protestantism was wholly permissive, a weakening of the resistance to the supposed amoralism of economic development. While for Weber, the development from Calvin to late Protestantism was neither only nor essentially an adaptation to change in external circumstances. It concerned an unfurling of the latent implications of the religious position itself.[5] Tawney, in short, was the supporter of ethical rigor opposed to economic individualism. For him, the development of this individualism coincided with the collapse of certain moral standards. He saw Calvin as a "modern mind" who had absorbed much of lay Renaissance culture and thus was more receptive than Luther to the needs of economic development. Tawney in essence saw Protestantism as a relaxation to which other branches of Christianity or a new lay morality should react. According to him, late Puritanism was favorable to individualistic positions not by reason of its internal positions, but as a result of external economic and political developments. To Weber, on the other hand, if it were true that ascetic Protestantism offered a new model which abolished many old restrictions, it imposed at the same time a new rigorousness (active work, productivity). Tawney is closer to Spencer, Weber closer to Durkheim (the concept of "organic solidarity").

The examination of Tawney's foreword to *The Protestant Ethic and the Spirit of Capitalism* may be useful for a comparison of his and Weber's work.[6] Here, Tawney sets out Weber's thought synthetically. The problem is this: what were the psychological conditions which made the development of capitalist society possible? Weber, speaking of capitalism as a modern phenomenon, rejects the conventional responses (economic changes, acquisition instincts) with the aim of presenting it as the result of movements unleashed by the religious revolution of the seventeenth century. He sees the rise of a class of parvenus which, invigorated by Calvin's doctrine, was capable of overthrowing the old ethical standards and transforming work into a spiritual goal.

Tawney then moves to the criticism of this idea. He begins the discussion by referring to the economic evolution of England which produced a fairly different idea. Then he examined the current situation of scientific thought on this matter. It is no longer so novel to interpret religious beliefs and social institutions as different expressions of a common psychological attitude. It is clear that religious doctrines are reflected in opinions around the social order and that custom due to contingent economic factors should be reflected in turn in religion. Nor can it be denied that there is a connection between Calvinism and certain attitudes toward social ethics (compare the influence of Calvinism in Holland and England). The link between religious radicalism and economic progress which other writers before Weber had suggested but not developed thus seems obvious. More problematic is the *relation between Calvinist influence and other factors* on the development of capitalism. Weber devotes his essay only to the role of religious movements in creating conditions favorable to capitalist development. However, he said, until the role of the other factors (trade, finance, industry) is established, it is hard to estimate the importance of the former—adding that Calvinism and the spirit of capitalism could both be the results of specific economic changes. Weber was reproved for falling into the common error of using an idea, fruitful in itself, as a key to solve all the problems, as a unique principle for explaining complex phenomena. He is too subtle in attributing to intellectual or moral causes phenomena caused by more prosaic and mundane causes, which appear wherever there are determinate external conditions, independent of the dominant religious credo.

The analysis of intellectual and ethical forces in question also seems incomplete to Tawney. There are other analogous forces which Weber has not sufficiently considered (Renaissance thought, English economists), and the change in the economic ethic is also reflected in Catholic thought. Furthermore, Calvinist teaching was not unequivocal, as Weber described it, but underwent variations according to the countries and periods in which it developed. Weber was inspired by the works of the English Puritans of the second half of the seventeenth century. From these he drew the image of the pious Puritan bourgeois devoted to his business. However, the Calvinism of Geneva, Knox, the Presbyterians, the French Protestants, and the Pilgrim Fathers were all creators of collectivism and a rigid discipline. It is the *second*, individualist phase of Calvinism, which bears affinity to the "spirit of capitalism." Weber thus examined "not the conduct of Puritan capitalists but the doctrines of Puritan saints." If Weber enlightened us concerning the effects of religious ideas on economic development, says Tawney, it is no less important to state the reverse reaction—the effect of economic factors on what belongs to the religious sphere.

TAWNEY AND MAX WEBER

Let us therefore examine Tawney's work to see more closely his points of contact and difference with Weber's work. *Religion and the Rise of Capital-*

ism was published first in 1926, based on a series of lectures, "Religious Thought on Social Problems in the Seventeenth and Eighteenth Centuries," held at King's College, London, for the Holland Foundation in 1922.

A new edition in 1936[7] includes an author's preface: in this many of the themes in the foreword to *The Protestant Ethic* of 1930 are taken up again, although some hasty criticisms are corrected (such as that of Weber for not taking account of Renaissance thought). However, two criticisms remain firm: the exaggerated originality Weber attributed to Calvinism, and its stability and consistency in time and space. To Tawney, Weber studied one aspect: how religion affected men. He neglected the second: how social and economic changes affected religion. Weber had not studied the possible social needs which produced the Reformation, nor the causes, as well as the effects, of the religious mentality he analyzed. Tawney proposed saying something about "the influence exercised by economic expansion at the time on English religious thought."

The first chapter is dedicated to the "medieval heritage." The relationship between religion and economic life in the Middle Ages was one which desired the second subordinate to the first. Economic affairs should be subordinated to moral rules. Undoubtedly, in reality, this principle is difficult to realize. The first problem was provided by commercial activity— necessary for the public good though "dangerous for the soul," and suspect in that it was directed not at a just reward but at gain (greed for profit, hence the sin of greed and avariciousness). Merchants were tolerated, but with a series of restrictions: their activity should not aim at a profit higher than that necessary for their lives.

Another problem was that of usury, another necessary but highly culpable activity, from which a whole casuistry developed to distinguish the licit and the illicit in lending at interest. It is true that even the Church had recourse to this; but formally, it condemned it, above all in its most common form of the oppression by the rich of the poor, rather than in the forms of high finance.

Undoubtedly the practical behavior of the Church, and above all the ecclesiastical hierarchy, conflicted with what it preached (see too its attitude to serfdom). However, at least vices were recognized as such, and not, as happens today, transformed into virtues, where avarice has become economy and greed initiative, and the "natural law" has been replaced by the omnipotent principle of economic utility. This was not only hypocrisy. The summit of the Church was challenged. The poor Franciscan orders found themselves pitted against the pope. The reformers abominated the corrupt papacy precisely in the name of Christian principles.

In the second chapter, Tawney went on to analyze the "Reformers of Continental Europe." The religious revolution fell heavily on the economic revolution of sixteenth-century Europe. But it is wrong to interpret the fact that the religious movement not only coincided with the economic one but also in some way determined it. Capitalism—in the various meanings of the term—already existed when Christian thinkers still referred to the medieval economic ethic. "To believe that the rejection of religion in its primacy over economic activity and social institutions was contemporary with the revolt against Rome, means antedating a movement which finished only a century and a half later and was as much determined by changes taking place in economic and social organization as by developments in the sphere of religious thought."

In this period of economic expansion we witness a passionate anticapitalist reaction whose greatest representative is Luther, the "revolutionary conservative" who, before the disastrous consequences of economic development, preached the return to the simple life of the past. His revolt was against the laxity and corruption of authority, not against authority itself. He wanted to make the Church return to the old, simple society of believers. His concept was medieval, based on a vague "state of nature" (whose ideal lay in the life of the peasant). Luther accepted social hierarchy, but not its institutions. A basic incoherence marks his attitude. His refusal to externalize religion so as not to degrade it led him to impotence on the practical level. He thus asked of the state the duty of observing Christian morality. He was implacable against usury, even more than the Christian thinkers of the Middle Ages who preceded him. Strongly attached to the ethics of the past, he accepted the medieval doctrine but rejected its sanctions. He defended Christian morality but rejected its institutional framework.

Calvin, that modern soul, on the other hand, turned to an urban, industrial bourgeoisie, mostly made up of immigrants. It is mistaken to believe that he made many concessions to usury, but undoubtedly his attitude marks a shift in the religious conception of economic life. He is no longer the enemy of wealth, but only of its bad use. He completed a revolution in the traditional scale of ethical values. For the first time the so-called economic virtues made their appearance. Instead of returning to the past, like the Lutherans seeking refuge in the old values, or looking to the future like the humanists who saw humanity redeemed by the advent which triumphed over superstition and violence, Calvin looked for a third way by overturning the old taboos.

The two main elements of his doctrine were the importance ascribed to the responsibility, discipline, and asceticism of the individual, and commitment to embody Christian character in institutions. However, Calvinism varied from country to country, and from one time to another, according to the political climate, social classes, and above all whether his followers were a majority or minority in society. Thus the version of

Calvinism diffused in England was more individualistic, while New England saw a dictatorship of ministers who repressed trade and imposed the maximum social discipline on the state-church—closer, overall, to Calvin's Geneva than to the English Puritanism of the time. The government of Geneva was in fact marked by rigid discipline, sobriety, and the conflict between the clergy and the Council regarding the problem of commerce and usury (as the bourgeoisie easily accepted the imposing of sobriety but not commercial restrictions).

The third chapter is devoted to the Church of England. After examining the economic situation of England at the Reformation, especially the agrarian question, Tawney went on to examine the developments in religious theory which, he stated, was not capable of holding back the social reality of the time. While individualism showed itself powerful through economic development, religious doctrine continued its traditional teaching, which condemned injustice, oppression of the poor, and usury—the latter the central point from the Middle Ages to the Reformation, of the economic ethic of the Church, and which included under the term usury every form of economic pressure, of a contrast disadvantageous for one of the parties, or profit due to the simple lending of capital. However, these condemnations had lost their efficacy. On the one hand, the Church had always accepted social hierarchies. On the other, Calvin had opened up a gap by showing himself tolerant to usury, so that to some extent the guarantee of religion was also given to juridical laws. The silence of the Church in the face of the phenomenon of the "industrial revolution" and the "horrors of the first factories" is explained by a century of passivity and acquiescence.

In the last chapter we arrive thus at the Puritan movement. At the end of the sixteenth century, Tawney stated, the separation between religious theory and economic reality was already clear. However, meanwhile, religious theory itself was maturing, ready to revolutionize traditional values and the doctrine of social obligations. The principal currents developed in England from Calvin's thought were Presbyterianism, Congregationalism, and Puritanism. The last was the most widespread, penetrating and powerful, and it permeated not only theology but also society. "Puritanism was the teacher of the English middle classes." The Puritans tried to give a schematic formulation to economic ethics: "a pious discipline against the religion of commerce." Among its champions was Richard Baxter. Theirs was an attempt to formulate a "Christian casuistry of economic morality," an attempt made also by Catholics at one time. But they were even less successful than the latter. This lack of success was due not only to external circumstances. Its roots lay in the very heart of Puritanism. The capitalist spirit was not a result of Puritanism, but it did find a tonic in certain aspects of late Puritanism. The second spirit of Puritanism was revealed only when favorable economic and social conditions allowed it to develop. Thus Calvin's doctrine, from being the creator of authoritarian regulation, became the vehicle of individualism and underwent a profound transformation. Thus in England some accused Calvin of being the father of licence while others applauded the commercial enterprise of Calvinist communities and their freedom from antiquated prejudices regarding economic morality.

The two elements in Calvin's doctrine—approval of economic enterprise and at the same time rigid discipline—split in English Puritanism, and the collectivist aspect disappeared while the individualistic one triumphed. In Calvin, there was "a circumspect concession to practical needs." In his followers, this was transformed into an idealization of the trader's life. Thus we see the "triumph of economic virtues" whereby to be good Christians meant also being clever in business.

Typical of this change was the manner in which the problem of enclosures was dealt with: first condemned as the result of greed and oppression, and then encouraged as economically useful to the private sphere, and thus to society (as well as forcing the peasants to work in a disciplined fashion under the owner's eyes, thus elevating them morally), and pauperism. Aid to the poor was now the object of reproof. Poverty was due to idleness. The idea of a social responsibility for it did not appear. Economists and religious moralists helped each other to view aid to the poor, high wages, and welfare as morally pernicious and economically ruinous. The last sections of Tawney, while recognizing the merits of Puritanism regarding political freedom, are fierce in this regard. His condemnation of this economic ethics is total. Finally, Tawney's argument is distinct from Weber's in that he believed English Puritanism, though having at the start certain of its own characteristics (collectivism, rigor, and discipline but in a social sense) was then influenced by the development of capitalism, and sacrificed its own ethic to its need for development, though having in this "functional form a considerable influence on the development of capitalism." He thus accuses Weber of having ignored the influence of economic and social conditions on capitalism. Tawney further stresses more the "character" which religion molds and which he considered important for the development of capitalism, rather than its regulation (the method of ascetic life).

FROM THE "ACQUISITIVE SOCIETY" TO THE "FUNCTIONAL SOCIETY"

Tawney was called by Hugh Gaitskell, secretary of the Labour Party, the democratic and socialist philosopher par excellence. What does this mean, aside from the obvious celebratory intention? It is hard to reply fully to this without referring to the principles Tawney established and tried to demonstrate abundantly with historical references and juridical considerations in his first, most committed book of political essays, *The Acquisitive Society* (1921). However, as a start, and leaving aside the book's major arguments, one must raise the problem of what it means to be a political philosopher in England. It seems to me that in English culture more than in any other, the political philosopher is constantly held back, as it were. By his radical nature, his progress with clear logic to the point of madness to extreme conclusions (like Saint-Just), he very quickly meets unsurmountable barriers. However radical he may be or believe he is, there is no political philosopher in England in whom there is not at least an ounce of Burkean minimalism for whom the supreme virtue of the activist and thinker in politics is "prudence." Tawney did not escape, and indeed in many important aspects embodied, Edmund Burke's teaching: his distrust for abstract revolutionary projects, the deep—as it were, congenital—hostility for the dogmas of political theory, the hostility which lies at the base of his ferocious criticisms of the French Revolution (for which, see Burke's remarkably pertinent *Reflections on the Revolution in France* which so amazed Thomas Jefferson and had the effect of unleashing Marx's biblical anger).

In what sense, therefore, should Tawney be considered a "democratic and socialist philosopher"? In my view, Tawney was a philosopher in the sense that he tried to clarify the distinction between the ends desired and the practical situation—that is, the limits of tolerance of the real, social, and political forces, working on the immediate practical level, as regards the plans for transforming existing relations of strength and the conflicts of interest which ensued. In other words, he is a philosopher to the extent in which, as against the politician immersed in the immediate and the everyday, he exalted the demand for strategy. He never tired of proclaiming the validity and need of this, but was careful not to confuse the two levels, the tactical and the strategic—not to fall victim to "dialectical impatience," not to gloss over the difference between what by definition is always desirable and what is historically possible given the specific circumstances. Tawney's "philosophical" contribution must be seen in this perspective, or in that of a reformism which is not one of surrender, certainly, but is at the same time alien to any more or less abstractly doctrinaire Jacobinism. That later this outlook allowed many politicians, Labour or not, to placate their consciences and accept the postponement of the great revolutionary transformations indefinitely to better days, and Tawney himself to accept posts and responsibilities which ended up making him a pillar of the British establishment, is a question which has no important results at the really theoretical level of the framework of research, but rather involves and bears upon the bio-graphic fortunes of individuals.

In Tawney, the "acquisitive society," based on money and generally on pecuniary relations and a spirit of accumulation which often touches on theft, is contrasted with "functional society." The terms used by Tawney to define "acquisitive society" are still basically linked to the world of thought which develops from Adam Smith into Hayek. The inspiration and style of functioning of the basic institutions of this society do not concern the performance of tasks linked with the needs of "public service," but rather tend to clear the ground so that private enterprise can develop to its fullest extent. He said: "If one were to ask what is the goal or criterion of social organisation, one would reply by recalling the formula of the greatest happiness for the greatest number. However, to state that the aim of social institutions is happiness, is the same as stating that these institutions have no common aim. In fact, happiness is individual, and to place happiness as the object of society means dissolving society itself into the ambitions of an infinite number of individuals, each directed towards achieving some personal goal. These societies can be called acquisitive, as their orientation, interest and concern lie in promoting the acquisition of wealth."[8]

Tawney's criticism of this type of society takes on a tone more moralistic than scientific. I mean that, while Marx or Veblen, to cite two thinkers who at times developed similar arguments to Tawney's, criticizes capitalist society (Marx) and the society of the robber barons (Veblen), in terms of the systemic contradictions whereby both the Marxist capitalist society and Veblen's business society would not in the long run escape the crisis and collapse which seemed linked to their inner mechanism, Tawney sets up his own critique around a somewhat moralizing criterion. In fact, he found that in the prevailing mental climate of acquisitive society, men "do not become religious, or sages, or artists; religion, art and wisdom in fact imply the acceptance of limitations. Rather, they become powerful and rich."[9] It is therefore clear that Tawney's reservations regarding acquisitive society are essentially moral: that is, they concern the quality of life and the type of personality this society needs and which it inevitably ends up by creating. For these reasons, it should not be too surprising that the main argument which serves as foundation for the whole *pars destruens* of Tawney's thought may essentially be reduced to the idea of "privilege." In his view, there is privilege in society when "there is no function corresponding to a right." The moralistic character of this principle emerges clearly in the simple fact that it is stated as a self-evident principle beyond any determination in space and time, or by removing it from historical specificity. For Marx, it was private ownership of the means of production in the bourgeois era which excited the contradictions which, through the simultaneous raising of production to maximize profit and the contraction of consumption due to low wages, was supposed to bring the system to its final collapse. For Veblen, the contradiction began, sharpened, and finally exploded in the permanent tension between the captains of industry in the true sense, concerned with production and rational calculation, functionally oriented and ready to reinvest in technical innovation, and the captains of business, ever ready to scent the opportunity of making money independently of, or even contrary to, the needs of the productive apparatus—manipulators of money but absolutely incapable of rational calculation, robbers rather than planners, owners of parasitic income rather than holders of productive roles. In Tawney there was no lack of stinging criticism of the essential parasitism of many social figures, legitimated on the basis of the system of natural rights. The very concept of "functional society" stood on the premise that the legitimation of social roles, of technical-functional patterns, and consequent positions of relative advantage, should be sought exclusively in the contribution these roles brought to the welfare of the community. His polemic against the absentee landlord and shareholder recalls in more than one place that of Veblen, but he rarely managed to establish as a real target a real, compelling process in the social structure which might derive from a truly expansive voluntarism, but one not cognitively binding. One cannot conclude from this that Tawney's teaching ends up in a purely pedagogic function, or in an exhortatory declamation, a kind of Mazzinian typology of "rights and duties." The penetrating nature of many individual analyses connected with the functioning of industry or the inadequacy of political representation, the very distrust of the abstraction of traditional socialist literature and the outspoken polemic against doctrinaire ideology, make his work frequently exemplary, while still maintaining today a degree of noteworthy relevance.

NOTES

1. In an obituary of Tawney by Parsons, in "The Profession: Reports and Opinion," *American Sociological Review*, vol. 27, n. 6, 1962, p. 888.

2. A. Crosland, *The Future of Socialism*, New York: Macmillan, 1957.

3. See H. Luthy, *Le passé présent, combats d'idées de Calvin à Rousseau*, Monaco: Éditions du Rocher, 1965.

4. J. D. Chambers, "The Tawney Tradition," *Economic History Review*, vol. 24, No. 3, 1971, pp. 355–69.

5. See Parsons, "The Profession," p. 888f.

6. M. Weber, *The Protestant Ethic and the Spirit of Capitalism*, trans. by T. Parsons, New York: Scribner's, 1930, 1958.

7. R. H. Tawney, *Religion and the Rise of Capitalism*, London: John Murray, 1936.

8. R. H. Tawney, *The Acquisitive Society*, London: Bell, 1921, p. 32.

9. Tawney, *The Acquisitive Society*, p. 333.

10

+

Werner Sombart: Genesis, Characteristics, and Contradictions of Modern Capitalism

A BOURGEOIS *MALGRÉ LUI*

Overshadowed by the greater fame of Max Weber and, like Weber, obsessed by the great ghost of Marx, Werner Sombart is a contradictory, controversial, and fascinating figure in the history of economic and social thought. A certain grouping of tensions and ambivalences, if not of real ambiguities, was already recorded in his biographical data and family origins. He was born into an entrepreneurial family, linked to the logic of the development of aggressive nineteenth-century capitalism in its phase of accelerated accumulation; moreover, it was socially aware, and topics like class struggle, the *sociale Frage*, and the martial laws of Kaiser Wilhelm I were openly discussed, even though there was a tendency to temper intellectual lucidity with judicious doses of the "sense of opportunity." His father was a landowner, solid, already wealthy, who faced the new era with prevision. That he was already a well-established bourgeois may have allowed him that critical distance as regards immediate class interests which is the basic condition for producing mid- and long-term fruitful investments. It is a fact that the elder Sombart, by intelligent reconversion, before the dramatic extent of the fall of traditional agricultural income was fully manifest, industrialized agriculture, radically modified his own business and showed himself to be an enlightened employer: that is, socially aware and at the same time technically trained.

It is not surprising to find him among the founders of the famous Association for Social Politics, politically and ideologically close to the so-called Socialists of the Chair, meticulously and often even pedantically

103

positioned like typical Social Democrats as regards reform, who were seen as having the task less of structural transformation of society than the more modest one of helping capitalism pragmatically overcome its own internal conditions.

His social and family origins are brought up not because they mechanically and exhaustively explain an entire individual destiny—which perhaps in its central, essential core was to be a singular, nonreductive, unrepeatable fact. These are referred to because they provide the framework, the picture of conditions within which Sombart was growing. However, one point is preliminary, but basic: Sombart speaks of "bourgeois" and "bourgeoisie;" he does not speak from hearsay but from direct knowledge.

ANALYST AND ACTOR

The picture of the "bourgeois" he presents to us in all his writings, but especially in the book which bears this title (*The Bourgeois: The Quintessence of Capitalism*), is not only the product of long hours in the library and the archives. It is also a portrait of the subject from within. Later, when there was a discussion of its "artistic" nature—so light as to come close to untenable contradictions, to have endangered in more than one circle his respectability as the Herr Professor—it would be necessary to cite at least one extenuating factor. Sombart found himself in the uncomfortable position of being at the same time analyst and actor. When he was writing about the bourgeoisie, his restless and rather maniacal activism, his perpetual state of dissatisfaction—all trace the physiognomy of an historical social type, but also plumb the depths of himself, drawing for us a self-portrait.

By simple association of ideas and with no empirical support, his case reminds me of Engels, who, however, should be accorded a sounder knowledge and a stronger logic. But Engels could count on Marx. Yet it is true that at the same time Engels worked with Marx on elaborating "scientific socialism," he also managed his father's textile firm in Manchester. In his father's business, Engels every day studied the concrete, lived development of capitalist relations of production and, together with a few eagerly awaited sovereigns, sent Marx his empirical observations. It is my belief, based on the leaps of syntax and style, that the chapters of the first volume of *Capital* on mechanization and big industry, and the working day appear so distinct from the rigorously philosophical and "dialectical" progress of the initial chapters (remember the dialectical circle which opens the first: commodity-money-commodity), for the simple reason that those chapters owe much to Engels's collaboration and his characteristic "sociological" positivism.

The young Sombart was of delicate health. This not only saved him from the world of business, to which the family naturally wished to tie him, but helped him also to escape to the South, to Italy. This choice was far from original; plenty of young Germans with high hopes descended from the northern mists to seek out the clean air and mild climate of Italy. Sombart studied at Pisa and Rome. He devoted his graduating thesis to what was then the most poetic of countrysides—the Roman. The first scientific work Max Weber wrote was also—under the supervision of Mommsen—dedicated to a discussion on Roman history (the relations between the forms and techniques of land measurement and the public and private juridical relations to which they were subjected in classical Roman antiquity). This is not a chance occurrence, or parallel. It is but an example of that deep, brilliant, passionate tradition of classical studies and classical philology which sought its outlet in Rome in the Wilhelmine era, emerging from German universities, and which, besides Mommsen and the whole Historical School, had its illustrious forerunners in Wincklemann, the *Roman Diaries* of Gregorovius, and Goethe's *Travels in Italy*.

Sombart finished his thesis and at twenty-six was appointed adjunct professor of economics in Breslau University. He was to finish his career as a professor emeritus, but his was a career full of accidents, which possibly only the shock-absorber of his family origins stopped from being a failure. His reputation as a "red professor," which simply indicates a number of nonconformist attitudes, rather than a conscious and coherent revolt against the status quo, followed him and indeed preceded him everywhere, helping to deny him the title of full professor. Certainly, it would be wrong to make a martyr of him, but it is true and worth remembering that Sombart's contribution was basic in putting Marx's thought and work into circulation into the German university world, for which for a time he was ostracized by the German academic authorities. Furthermore, with Nazism firmly seated in power, it was Sombart who signed *Vom Menschen*, in 1938, a partly miscellaneous anthropological manual, but at the same time one of the few, if not the only, work published in Germany during the years of full consolidation of Nazism in which the premises of the theory of the "master race" were explicitly criticized as untenable.

RELATIONS OF PRODUCTION AND VALUES

What is today still valid, of the quantitatively massive production of Werner Sombart? Or, in other terms and perhaps with more relevance as regards the current need for a critical revision: what is the kernel, the emerging problem of Sombart's thought? And what today is the level of immediacy of this emerging problem?

An adequate response to these questions is neither easy nor simple. In my view, this difficulty is linked to the internal characteristics of his thought and certain peculiarities in its presentation. There is no doubt about the brilliance, often abundant, of the writer. However, what one gains in stylistic liveliness and also in agility and nimbleness in the elaboration of his thought, runs the risk of being lost because of the scant systematic nature of the approach. The intuitive-artistic nature of many passages in Sombart here reach their insurmountable limit. He was certainly a serious scholar, but he gave his best, not by chance, in a monograph like *The Bourgeois*, rather than in a multivolume work like *Modern Capitalism*, intended to be systematic and definitive, but instead is stodgy and uneven in many places. His nature, divided between the fire of poetic intuition and the controlled—and inevitably a little gray— seriousness of the erudite makes one think of him as a kind of Tonio Kroeger of social thought: too scholarly to give in to the impulses of inspiration but also too "Mediterranean" not to suffer from its subtly painful fascination.

However, whoever glances at Sombart's work, notwithstanding the reservations which may be suggested by recent research or the flights of fancy of certain of the author's judgments, will soon see the high degree of relevance and thus the abiding interest of the essence of Sombart's thought. The central problem on which Sombart patiently— though not always—went on gathering data, documentation, and ideas is still our problem today. What is the relationship of relations of production of a capitalistic type to modern society, viewed as a global reality of structure, culture, personality, motivations, and values? In other words, what are the relationships which occur between economy, morality, religion, ideology, and orientations in society as a whole? Where does it take its deepest motivations from, and also its real legitimation, the dominant style of life?

To describe the problem is sufficient to evoke the names of at least two great contemporaries, Marx and Weber. In fact, the similarities among the three scholars are considerable. Certain basic themes are common to all three. Also, some conclusions seem to be in common, with different emphases, especially as regards the structural and functional difficulties of the capitalist system which, if for Marx historically concern the objectively, historically embodied contradiction in class struggles, for Weber and partly also for Sombart involve a question summed up in the formula of the "bureaucratization of social relations and life," and which seems to be located beyond capitalism and socialism, in that it involved them both.

Whether we accept it or not, Sombart's originality thus emerges very distinctly. As regards Marx, Sombart is clearly distinguished by his insistence on the "spirit" of capitalism: that is, its mentality, values, and orientations which lie at the basis of the genesis of the capitalist world. In a page of *Modern Capitalism*, which recalls the celebration of the bourgeoisie to which Marx and Engels devoted themselves in the *Manifesto*, Sombart's words take on a dithyrambic note: "Capitalism was born from the depths of the European spirit." It is thus, with a brilliant formulation that the whole theoretical Marxist construct, which hinges on the objective conflict into which there necessarily enter human beings as a result of their material means of life, is simply, and fairly simplistically, obliterated. However, Sombart goes on to describe that same spirit not only as the source of the new state and the new religion, as well as the new science, but also that which creates the new economic life. It is an earthly spirit, a mundane one, both hugely destructive in regard to past formations and at the same time able to construct new forms of life.

THE LIMITS OF TECHNICAL PROGRESS

At this point, it would be sufficient if Sombart in some way had clarified the origin of this splendidly creative "spirit." Sombart did it with a literary reference—in truth, rather too cheaply. He called it the spirit of Faust, of unrest and anxiety which now animates man and which is also beginning to dominate economic life.

In this regard, it would be hard to deny the influence on Sombart of another great German sociologist, his contemporary, Max Weber. Especially in *The Protestant Ethic and the Spirit of Capitalism*, but also in his famous studies on ethics in world religions,[1] Weber masterfully brought out—if not always with sufficient dialectical logic—the subtle links which, beyond the awareness of historically acting agents, bind a specific lived ethic to a given economic system, with its rules, organizational structures, and psychological and value motivations. Not only this: common to both is the conviction that the modern world is necessarily a "disenchanted" one, dominated by the iron laws of formal rationality, tending toward universal bureaucratization and the commodification of all interpersonal relations.

However, what appears in Weber as the bare, scientific construction of a link between methodical or "holy" life, and the reinvestment and hence the reproduction of capital, is changed in Sombart and takes on a note of strong moral condemnation. Alongside the innovative moment in the capitalist spirit, to Sombart there is also developing a "bourgeois spirit." If the entrepreneurial spirit wished to earn, to conquer, the bourgeois spirit wished to command and preserve. In other words, the bourgeois spirit is the consolidation of capitalism, its complete institutionalization, but also the confirmation of its negative characteristics, the acceptance of money as supreme value and criterion of judgment.

Sombart's reasoning and analysis are here reunited and refer us back to the important *Philosophy of Money* of Georg Simmel, which in many crucial aspects anticipated the demystifying critique of the Frankfurt School as regards mass culture. On the other hand, the pages Sombart devoted to the aspiration to money and thus the maximization of profit and the conversion of money and profit into power—economic, political or social— are still pages of extraordinary vitality, and serve to illuminate phenomena which are part of our everyday experience.

While agreeing with Weber's methodological outlook (the famous value-freedom, or *Wertfreiheit*, on whose significance in Weber and Sombart I cannot dwell here), Sombart diverged from Weber over the innovatory role of the Protestant ethic: for Weber it is basic as "sanctifying" systematic labor with the mediation of *Beruf* (both religious vocation *and* profession), while for Sombart it is involutive, with its emphasis on "sacrifice"—Sombart's position deepening little by little to the point of changing into a real counterposition. Max Scheler grasped this conflict very well: "Max Weber brings out in the new system of Protestant life and doctrine . . . one of the prime moments of the unlimited tendency-to-work; . . . and, what is much more important from a psychological point of view, he explains that the urge to make money is but a simple manifestation accompanying the first impulse to work without end and its ethico-religious sanctification, as 'duty' understood in the ascetic sense. Sombart, on the other hand, believes that the impulse to make money is a new, prime element as regards the new impulse to work, and shows that in the Thomist doctrinal system the first justification of a purely worldly tendency to make money, independent of the search for salvation, is provided."[2]

Scheler ends up agreeing with Weber. Sombart's reading of Thomism does not seem to him sufficiently critical. Sombart, in his view, "roughly releases the rational ethic of the wholly organic laws of Thomism in this great, systematic expression of the ethico-Christian conscience of the late Middle Ages." This is not the place to resolve a dispute which is certainly not concluded in its philological terms. To have guessed at the limits of a society highly advanced from the technical point of view, but uncertain and egotistically divided regarding its ultimate goals, is perhaps, to me, the most solid claim of Sombart to a reconsideration at once critical and participant of his thought today.

NOTES

1. See, in this regard, my *Max Weber and the Destiny of Reason*, trans. by John Fraser, Armonk, N.Y.: Sharpe, 1982, and my "Introduzione" to the collection Max Weber, *Sociologia delle religioni*, 2 vols., ed. C. Sebastiani, Torino: UTET, 1976.

2. Max Scheler, *Vom Umsturz der Werte*, Leipzig: Peter Reinhold, 1919; Italian trans. by V. Filippone, in the anthology *La sociologia*, ed. F. Ferrarotti, Milano: Garzanti, 1974.

11

✝

Vilfredo Pareto: The Disenchanted World of Conservative Pessimism

AN INCONVENIENT CHARACTER

Born in 1848 in Paris, but into an old Genoan family; educated in mathematics and engineering, but exceptionally well versed in classical Greek and Latin literature; an industrial technician and manager, but at the same time a fully qualified university professor; a frank, explicit hater of politicians, still more of amateur politicians, but who, all the same, attempted a political career, Pareto was all in all an inconvenient character, hard to classify, who cannot be dealt with by a simple reference to any preconstituted category.

There is no doubt we are dealing with a complex personality in whom the conflicts and tensions which shook the European scene between the 1848 revolution and its rather too facile Messianism, and the catastrophic result of the First World War, seem precisely reflected. It was a period dominated by the romanticism of science, that kind of lay-religion of ingenuous Comtean positivism, ready to worship the facts, the specific realities, the ugly but concrete aspects of life, immediately observable beyond and against the claim of any purely conceptual direction or design, with a rapture so genuine and defenseless as to constantly risk creating the metaphysics of the antimetaphysical. It was to be Émile Zola who gave it an intuitive formulation, nonetheless more precise than those of the professional commentators and professors. "Metaphysical man is dead, the whole earth is transformed with physiological man."

At the same time, Pareto's age was socially and politically in decline, and knew itself to be so. In France, the country and culture to which he

111

was to stay so deeply bound, to the point of writing some of his basic works directly in French, this was the period of the Second Empire and Third Republic, marked by the advent of the process of industrialization on a massive scale, from the first great concentrations of bourgeois wealth, the administrative and political scandals, the disaster of Sedan and of the Dreyfus *affaire*. In Italy, unification took its first laborious steps. The conflicts of interest clash violently behind the rhetoric of Risorgimento. The closed, municipal cultures, which the law of 1859 simplistically tends to "Piedmontize," even at the cost of changing their nature or suffocating them, entered into collision with the idea of public interest, and strongly asserted the ancient ties of kinship and clientalism. Protectionists and laissez-faire exponents fought each other relentlessly to the point of the "tariff war" against France and the bloody repression of Bava Beccaris in Milan. Behind the disenchanted expressions of Pareto's realism which may nurture cynicism, one clearly sees the basic pessimism of the second half of the century in which faith in the automatic progress of the human species and the Enlightenment promises of a triumphant, universal rationality seemed wholly shipwrecked and betrayed. In Pareto, this pessimism is openly transformed into a bitter mockery of democratic and humanitarian ideals, seen as illusory, while in Weber and Durkheim, his two great contemporaries, this emerges with the deep, provocative pathos which accompanied the proletarianization of the spirit and the painful nostalgia for an organically combined humanity, sure of the unwritten rules without the need of religious sanction, dominated not by individual hedonistic caprice, but the ethical imperatives of the great social institutions.

There is a whole "structure of feelings" for which the development of capitalism left no space, and which it needed the First World War to destroy, preceded only by the lonely, unheard warning of Nietzsche. These were the years in which liberal European civilization entered into crisis definitively: its written rules and still more its norms of fair play which, as a powerful backing of every positive law, still remained invisible, a genuine *esprit des lois*, which could not be made explicit. This was a society "from the top," with a narrow, fragile social base, in whose context nations recognized and identified themselves in their own elites, which are first eaten away at the roots, forced to atrophy, and then swept away by mass industrial society, finding a monetary, authoritarian, illusory defense of their own sectoral interests and privileges in Fascism and Nazism.

This was a disenchanted attitude, a basic pessimism regarding the perfectibility of human nature: with an undeniable, fascinated attraction for force and its use in social questions—the idea that history was made by elites and only by them, and moreover was no more than a graveyard of aristocracies. One must add, the profound distrust of any reasoning not immediately linked to proof, an extreme empirical concern, a horror of faith of any kind, the constant concern of "falling into pure ideology"—in outline, here are the characteristics of the psychological and intellectual "identikit." Naturally, this is a somewhat crude simplification. An ardent temperament and so swift an intelligence must not be expected to experience a development without contradiction. However, the basic traits of Pareto's temperament became fixed through time.

His intellectual development has its places, its geography: Turin, Rome, Florence, Lausanne. However, it is the last two which had a decisive role. At the Turin Politechnico he followed the footsteps of his father, a hydraulic engineer, who, summoned from Paris to Italy like Quintino Sella, was to finish his career as president of the Upper Council for Public Works. After graduating, Pareto found work with the Roman railways, but this was a brief interlude, and one can imagine his disgust for an environment dominated by clientalism and personal recommendations. Then he went to Florence, by way of the friendly pressure of the director of the Banca Generale, Allievi, an infallible identifier of elites, as Pantaleoni described him, who had no hesitation in appointing Pareto, only twenty-five years old (1874), director of the Ferriere Italiane in Val d'Arno.

This was a position with a strictly technical responsibility, with precise operational, administrative commitments which caused him to travel through Europe, especially in Scotland and England; however, this engineer, endowed with a swiftness in his work which touched on pedantry, did not seem one to burn himself out in the routine of a profession. He was a young scholar, fiery, brilliant, who also frequented circles not directly connected with his professional world.

First, he was a constant guest of the Peruzzi salon, a center of interdisciplinary, avant-garde culture, where one could meet alongside the philologists Comparetti and Collodi (the author of *Pinocchio*), the Dante scholar Linaker and the physiologist Schiff, with a swarm of clever women in Stendhal's sense—such as the wife of Ubaldino Peruzzi, Emilia, Maria Pasolini, Angelica Rasponi, and Mrs. French—not to mention Sidney Sonnino, Giustino Fortunato, Gino Capponi, Francesco Ferrara, termed by Pareto the "prince of Italian economists," and many others.

For Pareto these were determining times and contacts. One must try to understand how Florence was then, so different from the dignified but also rather provincial isolation of today.

Florence then enjoyed the positive results of swift political and social change. A certain disorder rocked it: political and intellectual debate developed in a fervent, meticulous, and at times fierce manner. We owe to Maffeo Pantaleoni, loyal and faithful friend of Pareto throughout his life save for periods of coolness or misunderstandings, an overall picture of the situation in Florence of those years: "This was the period in which the problem arose whether the railway should be private or State: the time in which the Socialism of the Chair pervaded Italy and on the one hand Luzzatti, Lampertico, and Cossa made up a school of political economy in opposition to which Ferrara, Martello and the Johannis set up the Adam Smith Society, in Florence, and had the review *Economista* in Florence as outlet. This was the time that there was first discussed in an extensive manner what was later to be termed the question of North and South and Sardinia, and thus laissez-faire or protectionism, regional autonomy or centralization."[1]

FROM ECONOMICS TO SOCIOLOGY

There is thus nothing mysterious in Pareto's development, which, moreover, with that bit of narcissism which seems to characterize the timid but aggressive, provided some glimpse of the full details of his internal life and moral and political convictions. We have to take his word for it, that with peculiar precocity at the young age of sixteen he had already read two emblematic authors, the Bossuet of the "universal history," infused with metaphysical belief in Providence, and the Bastiat of the "economic harmonies," a proponent and theorist who was highly esteemed by economic liberalism of the most intransigent kind—and with this the game was over and his fate sealed. Bossuet displeased him "acutely" while his enthusiasm was stimulated for Bastiat as economist. The choice of the factual is clear, for the circumscribed, empirically (or "experimentally," as he was to prefer to say) analyzable, as against the philosophizing obscurities, the metaphysical tirades or great humanitarian ideals, behind which he always, and not always wrongly, detected an ideological intrigue or political trick.

The entire voluminous writings of Pareto,[2] but especially the letters from Antonucci, are precious documents. At twenty, Pareto said he had read and been seduced by Buckle. "My belief at the time was more or less this. Political economy, as the so-called classical economists have set it up, was a perfect or nearly perfect science. There only remained the process of putting its principles into practice. Thus there was needed an imitation of Cobden's league, which was more useful and which humanity could have had for centuries as a sublime order. In politics, sovereignty of the people was an axiom, freedom a universal panacea, history showed us on the one hand a good, honest intelligent populace oppressed by the upper classes, to whom superstition belonged. Militarism and religion were the worst scourges of mankind. Among the ancients,

Caesar, and the moderns, Napoleon I and III were for me kinds of crooks. I denied or at least excused the evils of democracy. The Terror was a slight stain on the bright picture of the French Revolution."[3]

Interest in the economic aspect, but also its social context and inevitable political relevance, thus began early in Pareto. Here was a sociologist in the making, and it is easy to understand the influence on him at the outset of the work of Comte and Spencer, variously but with similar force. The passage from mechanistic and mathematical economist to sociologist in the real sense is unquestionably interesting from a logical and interpretive point of view. How did one become ready to reject or, better, to recognize that the human world was not to be reduced to a mathematical formula, as in the case of the theorems of pure economics, or that social phenomena were poorly adapted to a translation into the rigorous but abstract terms of mechanical physics?

However, the idea of contrasting a young Pareto, wholly devoted to "pure" abstract mathematical reasoning, to an older one, who little by little discovered the "real" reality of social phenomena in all its multidimensional fullness, seems to me untenable. Rather, one must consider a certain cooling in his temperament, a kind of entropy, whereby his open, warm enthusiastic nature, for the period under discussion, was to become increasingly disenchanted, almost bitter, suffused with a basic pessimism and distrust as regards the human race—so deep-set and undefeatable as to make him prefer the company of cats more than of his neighbors. However, in the years around 1874 in Florence, according to him, this had not yet occurred, and one could only guess at it through warnings in certain brusque, burning invectives against colleagues, bureaucrats, politicizers, and so on. He wanted to be a serious engineer, well-trained and conscientious, yet there he was, forced to play at intrigue. He was submerged with "recommendations" not all of which, given the eminence of the sender, were easily put to one side. This type of pressure could make him furious. Usually he took on the "excellent" applicants who were recommended, but then placed them at the same level as all the others, harshly, with no special attention, or exceptions. The poor newly appointed employees complained bitterly, as expected, with their highly placed references. The latter returned the complaints, duly expanded, to Pareto who lost time, peace, and nerves.

However, the Florence period, with all its problems, was possibly the happiest one for our brave, nearly thirty-year-old engineer. If his main setting was Peruzzi's salon, there was no lack of other outlets for this "spirit" which, according to Pantaleoni, "arose from his unusual perspicacity and a real cordiality, which needed laughter and which was able to excite it at the level of wit."[4]

It is hard to believe him. The smile on the lips of the great unmasker of "derivatives," or those rationalizations with which men like to deceive themselves and others, was perhaps more one of sarcasm than optimistic benevolence. However, his successes in Florence continued thick and fast. He was elected a member of the Academia dei Georgofili, a society created and maintained principally by Ubaldino Peruzzi. Soon after, he became a member of the Adam Smith Society.

The most outstanding scholars of Florence were members of the Georgofili, and it soon became the center of the liberal opposition. Years later, Pareto confided to his friend Pantaleoni that he had managed to become a member of the Georgofili only through the protection of Peruzzi. In these confidences one clearly sees the bitter acerbity of the man who had had to leave Italy to obtain the full recognition of his own abilities without having to bow down to anyone, without having to accept any Mafia-like submission. One feels too the disappointment of the scholar whom the University of Florence had prevented from giving an unpaid elective course in the social sciences.

However, he had been committed to the Adam Smith Society, which was inspired by Francesco Ferrara and whose executive president was the omnipresent Ubaldino Peruzzi. Until he left Italy for Lausanne, this was the only scientific membership Pareto held and boasted of. Against the Paduan school of economics, whose great names were Luigi Luzzatti, Fedel Lampertico, and Luigi Coass, the Adam Smith Society fiercely defended the principles of economic liberalism and social individualism. The Paduan school on the other hand favored state intervention in welfare and other social services for workers. As well, they advocated investments, necessary for the indispensable social infrastructures and for those services which, though basic for any modern community, would never have attracted the interest of private individuals since their management by definition was unprofitable, if not a losing concern. The Adam Smith Society, opposed to any State intervention on whatever grounds, stated in its program that it "promotes, develops, diffuses and defends, the doctrine of economic freedoms as they were understood by its foresightful founder Adam Smith, and then elaborated and applied by the economists and governments which have adopted it."

The whole propagandist activity of Pareto in the Florentine period reflected these principles with great consistency. Indeed one could say he followed the political and economic news of the troubled years between 1870 and 1890 which saw the dissipation of the enthusiasm and illusions of the Risorgimento, the fall of the historic Right and the rise of the "social question," and that he commented with meticulous obstinacy on the decisions of the government and large industrial groups day by day as they were formed in the light of an economic liberalism and almost intolerant laissez-faire.

One must add that from Pareto's "chronicles" there shines forth the progressive disenchantment of the young man, the idealist ready to take up arms in the name of sacred principles and political ideals believed to be desirable, in favor of the mature Pareto, distrustful of "youthful theories" and ready to unmask the real naked truth by stripping it of its ideological gloss and self-interested rationalizations. This process began in Florence, and was carried out in contact with the specific problems provided by daily happenings, not deductively by solitary meditation on the great metaphysical problems. The question concerning the means and causes which dominated the major change in him, from the urgency of the Florentine years to the skeptical pessimism of the Swiss ones, must start from this place if one wishes an almost certain answer, and if one wishes to avoid the weaknesses of schematic counterpositions.

Having balanced the budget but also having reduced itself to a narrow elite, the Right fell in 1876 and was excluded from power. The immediate occasion for the fall of Minghetti and the Right was furnished by the problem of the railways: whether the state should take over all the railways and manage them itself, or not. Minghetti presented a bill which put the burden of this responsibility on the State. The bill was turned down and brought down the government too. This result was made possible by the "betrayal," as it was to be called, of the Tuscan friends of Pareto. Though part of the moderate group, Peruzzi and his Florentine friends refused to support the government and thus ensured its defeat in order to remain faithful to their programmatic anti-interventionism and defense of private enterprise. However, for Pareto, the question was not only one of abstract principles: he knew the specific question of the railways from within, as a director general. He charged into the polemic with a series of articles, essays, and open letters in the *Economista*, the journal of the Adam Smith Society. The basic lines of his argument were neither brilliant nor particularly original. The industrial state is a contradiction. The railways were better off in the hands of private industry, since workers who are personally interested are inspired by the incentive of profit to sharpen their wits and not spare themselves.

FROM ONE CRISIS TO ANOTHER, THE *TRACTATUS* IS BORN

Liberalism and antistatism were so strictly held by him that in 1877 in the *Nuova Antologia* he attacked a bill trying to prevent some abuses carried out by the clergy. For him, this involved an unwarranted interference of the State in a question which was not its concern. While blocking State intervention, he did not, later, hesitate to ally himself with the socialists, who, however, he strongly criticized on the theoretical level. Yet the hope stimulated in the Florentine group and Pareto, especially after the fall of the "historic Right," weakened. The Left and its leader, Agostino Depretis, came out quickly in all their "transformism" and their insurmountable tendency to intrigue. These were the years in which Pareto as the bitter scourge of politicizers, "democracy," and humanitarian ideals was definitively formed. This seems to me incontestable.

The bitterness was tempered by humanistic studies which in Florence he could pursue with passionate application, especially when the duties of his job were lighter.

Aside from humanistic studies, there was still a broad margin for the "noble illusions" of a practical political kind. Indeed, in 1882 he moved toward militant politics. He who was later to mock politicians ceaselessly, to the point of seeing in them only wretched political hacks, decided to present himself as candidate in the elections of 22 November 1882, in the district of Pistoia; he was beaten.

His friend Pantaleoni was concerned to provide him with a rich selection of explanations from the general moralistic ones ("with the common people, charlatans and sophists count more than men of value") and from the more personal (if elected, he would have laudably carried on the great political traditions of the family, but his studies would have suffered, and with that the whole national culture; hence one must be resigned even if, with his charm as an enchanting conversationalist in the salons of Florence, who knew what success might thereafter have come to him. . .). There is no doubt of the charm of the young industrial manager-scholar and aspiring parliamentarian. One only need glance at the portrait we have of the twenty-six-year-old Pareto, with his penetrating eyes and thick black beard, to convince us. But Pareto, after the electoral failure in Pistoia, did not try again. His experience, though radically different, recalls Max Weber's. They were not born politicians. A defeat was enough to put them *hors de combat*.

However, his combativeness as publicist increased, indeed, in tone and volume. His father died in the same year as his political exploit, and he continued to live in Florence with his mother and sister Cristina, little by little withdrawing from professional concerns and increasingly devoting himself to writing. He published articles and essays sparked by contemporary events, usually in specialist journals, not only Italian but also French and less often English (namely, *Rassegna di Scienze Sociali e Politiche, Giornale degli Economisti, Journal des Économistes, Revue des Deux Mondes, The Speaker, Pall Mall Gazette*). In these writings, there shone through, over and above immediate polemical concerns, basic elements of his thought, its gradual but logical deepening and its direction to the understanding of the basic mechanisms which regulate the functioning of the social system and to the attempt to define and express them rigorously, not merely ideologically or in an abstractly doctrinaire fashion.

Increasingly absorbed in his work, Pareto made an intimate friend of Maffeo Pantaleoni, who in 1891 sent him his *Principi di economia pura*, published two years earlier by Barbera, Florence. In the biography and intellectual development of Pareto, 1891 was a critical year. Its wider political and social context was also in motion. The crisis of the Crispi administration on 2 February opened the way for that of Di Rudini, with Luttazzi as minister of the Treasury and then also of Finance. Pareto hoped that the latter, the famous protectionist of the Paduan school, would, however, be an advance over Crispi. His collaboration with the *Giornale degli Economisti* became regular. His correspondence with Pantaleoni was a valuable source not only for Pareto's biography but for the reconstruction of the intellectual climate of the time. Especially, Pareto moved increasingly toward pure economics, worked out mathematically, and began to get to know at first hand the work of Léon Walras, the Lausanne mathematical economist, for whom Pantaleoni gave him a letter as he was leaving for Switzerland.

What is striking about him on this occasion too, was the passion with which he threw himself into his new studies. The *Principi* by Pantaleoni gave him the opportunity for a series of critical demands and doubts about "pure economics." As usual, he did not mince words. Reading Cournot, he admitted frankly to finding the method dangerous, as Cournot tended toward protectionism. He was unconvinced also by Walras: it required all Pantaleoni's friendship to make him swallow him—not bad, for the relentless critic of ideologies.

At all events, there remained grounded and basic differences. For example, to claim to measure with a curve the utility of a commodity seemed to him a gross mystification which prevented the perception of the real phenomena of exchange. What was it? Was Pareto the sociologist already dissatisfied with the mathematical formalisms, perfect but empty, and hastening to break the shell to uncover the real world of real men? Perhaps it was too soon, but his criticism of the hypothesis of *homo economicus* was full of sociological foresights.

Once the ice was broken, thanks to Pantaleoni's letter, he began an exchange of letters with Walras which led to the meeting between the two scholars at Clarens, in the canton of Vaud. The year after, he went to Paris, and in 1893 met James Bryce, one of Gladstone's ministers, a well-known historian and "political scientist" *avant la lettre*. There were days of painful tension: his sister, to whom he was much attached, died on 19 April 1893, of meningitis. Meanwhile, however, the good Pantaleoni continued writing for him to Walras suggesting him as worthy successor to the chair of political economy at the University of Lausanne when Walras should have to vacate it.

Pareto did not set much store by this, being by then convinced that luck was against him. Moreover, even after his gesture of agreement for a future nomination, the silence lasted so long that his pessimism seemed justified. When he had decided to think no more of it, one fine spring morning Eugene Ruffy, state counsellor for Public Education in the Canton of Vaud, and Professor George Favey, chancellor of the University of Lausanne, came to Fiesole to offer him the position left vacant by Walras. He informed its contriver, his friend Pantaleoni, and got down to work preparing both the course and the inaugural lecture, leaving at once for Lausanne, asking his friends on the *Giornale degli Economisti* to restrict themselves to making a brief announcement without commenting.

However, after only a few years, in 1898, having gone to Genoa to take up a considerable legacy left to him by his uncle Domenico, with typical imaginativeness he mulled over the pros and cons of giving up the chair and his professorial duties, and devoting himself to the study of sociology.

This discipline was still very far from attracting more than a passing interest. One sees this too in the letter to Pantaleoni where he describes his teaching duties at Lausanne, as he understood them: "I was asked here to teach, like my predecessor: 1) pure political economy; 2) applied political economy; 3) social economics. I decisively refused the last, just because the name could make one believe in socialist tendencies not my own. So I said: 'I shall teach the first two, but not the third which for me does not exist'."

When Pantaleoni asked him if he had by chance read the (basically) sociological work of Max Nordau, who then enjoyed a certain celebrity, he replied straight off that he had no time to read things not "directly useful" to his work. Yet, shortly after, in 1899, he started a course on "theoretical socialist systems" and the same year announced to the Faculty and Department of Education his decision to give up teaching to devote himself exclusively to the writing of a "sociological tractatus."

In 1900, aside from contacts with Georges Sorel and the polemic against the English economist Francis Edgeworth, his exchange in July and August with Benedetto Croce over the nature of economic phenomenon is worthy of note on account of its outcome. Indeed, it is one of the few polemical exchanges (perhaps the only one) in which a representative of the social sciences more than held his own against Croce. The "destroyer" of positivism and the philosophy of history, he dominated Italian intellectual life and shortly was to decree the end of sociology or, at most, the acceptance of it as an "inferior means" of intellectual life.

Meanwhile, Sorel invited him to Paris for a course at the École des Hautes Études Sociales, but when he returned to Céligny he found that his wife, Alessandra Bakunin, whom he married on 23 December 1889, had left the family home. There were months of pain and loneliness, which not even his encounter with the young Jeanne Régis, in 1902, could sweeten. However, he applied himself ever more fiercely to the preparatory work for his *Trattato*: one might say this was the only therapy he had. An important witness to his state of mind is the letter to Pantaleoni of 15 February 1902: "If I should die, I should inform you I have designated you as my executor, and that my will is deposited with the notary Rochat, Lausanne, Rue de Bourgs."

One sees from the correspondence with Pantaleoni that, from time to time, Pareto saw himself as finished, and indeed wrote that he would like to live out his remaining years "doing nothing." In fact, all the while maturing in him was the grandiose design of the *Trattato di sociologia generale*, in which are amassed—apparently in disorder, or better, very precisely even though in a chaotic state from the point of view of form—all his lived experience from that of engineer and industrial manager to those of the militant publicist, economist, and lover of history and literature, avidly curious and fascinated by the political and social problems of the day.

The crisis was real: he decided to live openly with Jeanne Régis, but one can imagine, after all, the scruples and worries of this nineteenth-century— indeed, Victorian—professor. He also sent a letter of resignation from the chair which was rejected. Then there came an unexpected peaceful passage. The University of Bologna invited him to give a course in sociology. It was a fine reward. Meanwhile he worked furiously without letting himself be distracted or misled, like one who has little time ahead of him. The material for the *Trattato* grew apace. Every so often, as in the case of *Le mythe vertuiste et la letterature immorale* (1911), a whole part of the *Trattato* took shape and was sent off, published in anticipation and independently of the rest of the magnum opus. This finally saw the light in Florence in 1916, in two volumes, 1,700 pages, 2,612 paragraphs.

SOCIAL EQUILIBRIUM AND
THE USELESSNESS OF REVOLUTION

What is the kernel of his thought? What group of concepts characterizes it specifically? What today still stands of this undoubtedly grand but also cloudy construct?

It has been rightly observed that the commentators and critics, also harsh, have been many, but yet rarely have they managed to give a balanced comprehensive judgment of him.[5] It is useless to say that in Pareto's work itself there are all the excuses: a complex work with undeniable leaps in style, at times necessarily confused, which lent itself easily to the selective prejudices of individual readers. What one can say at once, even before entering into the details commonly seen as complex and complicated, is that Pareto is certainly not a Voltairean thinker.[6]

It is not that he lacked the mocking tone or the iconoclastic stance. He had an abundance. However, he was too disenchanted. Voltaire's battle was carried on with quite a different temper of pessimism. It was, as it were, a positive pessimism, dominated by the wish to create, construct. In a word, Voltaire's was an act of faith—certainly against traditional faiths, but still an act of faith, precise, sure of itself, and the repository of rational power, with all the enthusiasms and hopes that acts of faith entail: *Il faut dire la vérité et s'imoler*.

For Pareto the argument was different. In all his theories there was a more or less explicit attack on the faculties of man as rational being. His basic distinction between logical and non-logical actions, surprisingly detailed and so meticulously defined as to reach the limits of baroque engineering; of the residues and derivations, from which may be drawn the idea of man as ideological or tale-telling animal, tirelessly engaged in deceiving himself and others; the theory of the circulation of elites itself, with its underlying pessimism and which seems to mean that, all in all, history has nothing to teach save that efforts, however heroic, to change social situations, are simply useless—all show Pareto's much more radical pessimism, a disenchantment so total as to destroy the space for any illusion of qualitative, real changes. His motto might be *plus ça change, plus c'est la même chose*.

Perhaps it is here that the kernel of his thought should be sought. It seems difficult to me to see him simply as the sharp unmasker of ideologies as Norberto Bobbio has said often and with great interpretative finesse.[7] "By this one should not draw a veil over the theory of social equilibrium, but simply transfer the attention of new readers, especially those of the younger generation, to the theory and criticism of ideologies, which is a treatment which stands by itself and is susceptible to further development."[8] I have some doubts about the legitimacy of this "transferral." It is good to revive interest in the classics by bringing out particular aspects of particular immediate interest, but not at the cost of the basic positions. This would also be too convenient. However, in Pareto's case, this would force us to neglect or blind us to the extremely important link which undoubtedly exists between his work as unmasker and demystifier of rationalizations and false consciousness (as relentless and subtle as to recall Marx) and his basic pessimism, which places him in a position antithetical to Marx and brings one back necessarily to his logically conservative political choice.

It is almost unnecessary to stress that this choice inevitably recalls the theory of social equilibrium, the circulation of elites, as well as the theorization of the constant importance of force in regulating social relations.

This is not the place for a full investigation of these summary remarks, but I well know that the theory of social equilibrium in Pareto's thought, once examined and placed in its rightful position, the central one, immediately opens the door to claim Pareto for the functionalist school in one of its various versions. This attempt is particularly strongly proposed in Fiorot's fine monograph.[9] Here, Pareto, with the aid of Joseph Lopreato's interpretation, is considered an exponent, not merely a forerunner, of modern functionalism. This, if I see it rightly, is the current of sociological thought which, its variants aside, whether socially critical or conservative, finds a "system" in human society whose parts and "functions" are—always and universally—equally necessary and indispensable, in that it constantly and naturally tends toward a state of equilibrium according to the "laws" of homeostatic models. The corollaries of this interpretation are obvious. First, Pareto is absolved of the criticisms of psychologism which were never lacking, if only because he invoked too often, even if only metaphorically, the "instincts" (force, cunning) as a reserve, a residue, of human action in society. On this point, Fiorot agrees with my interpretation, save by adding that my rejection of the idea of a functionalist Pareto seems baseless: "[Ferrarotti] stresses that the logic of the social system as understood by Pareto, and the method of scientifically expressing and explaining its movements, are resolved in essentially mechanistic terms, strictly analogous to economic reasoning of a mathematical type . . . it does not then seem too difficult to recognize in the Paretan social system a considerable if not a complete openness to a structural-functional interpretation of social action, in that this system is presented as an interrelated and interdependent whole of reciprocally conditioning functions, and that in their ensemble, they make up the real social process."[10]

However, I do not deny this "openness," and even a certain "functionist" or even "organicist" tone in Pareto. Rather, I am convinced that the interpretation which wishes to find in him *all* the equipment of the structural-functional interpretation of social action does not stand up. This is for the very simple but basic reason I have already mentioned: "the interpretation in a functionalist sense of Pareto's system basically rests on the reduction of the concept of 'utility' to that of 'function.'" I noted elsewhere: "This type of reduction naturally makes possible a reading of Pareto not only as structural functionalist *avant la lettre*, but also leads to the discovery in him of the basic elements for mediating and to some extent joining together, if not exactly integrating, the two basic models of interpretation of society—that of integration-consensus, and that of coercion-violence. The reconstruction of his system on these interpretative lines is undoubtedly suggestive, even if the mechanistic approach, closed off from the historical-voluntarist interpretation of social action in the real sense, can appear in a more profound analysis to be an insurmountable limitation."[11]

The suggestion I raise of Pareto's mechanism seems disputable to Fiorot. "Essentially, Pareto's mechanicism does not rest on a reductive conception, which does not already imply the identical nature of the two phenomena but only the operational possibility of studying social phenomena *as if* they were physical-mechanical phenomena and at any rate the uniformities thus discovered are not held to be true because they conform to the mechanicistic model, but only when they appear as such at the moment of their verification against the facts."[12] The defense undertaken here of Paretan mechanicism is certainly ingenious, but aside from the fact that it seems far from convincing, it does not touch on the real problem which in my humble judgment lies in the limited "historical consciousness" of Pareto, despite his immense erudition in historical facts and anecdotes. It is hard to deny that history for him appeared as a great bubbling of triumphs and failures, fairly chaotic, of great and small and deceptive happenings, unattached to each other, without any global meaning, borne along, or, better, slowly cooked in a great pool of irrationality or at best of a-rationality in which nothing really happens and can happen.

Despite Bobbio's basically positive reactions, and the—at times—downright hagiography of Giovanni Busino, I continue to have serious doubts about Pareto's "historical consciousness." In this regard, possibly his language is a valuable key. The style is almost always clear, even colloquial. The punctuation is so loose as in some parts to touch on slovenliness. He seems not to know the correct use of period and comma, and even uses a comma where a clearer separation would be necessary. He had little sense of the paragraph and almost no interest in interpretations of the whole.

As regards substance, once he had expressed a general proposition, a relation between two phenomena, some part of "law," he had the habit of covering it, in the name of empirical proof, or, as he preferred to say, "experimental," with a mass of facts, historical examples, anecdotes, curiosities, and proverbs. In this regard, the inexhaustible mine for him was the history of classical Greco-Roman antiquity. Enjoyment was ensured, but the conclusiveness of the proof much less so.

However, there remains the full validity of the complex lesson of Pareto: first of all, the need for critical realism, or the need to go to the facts, the Machiavellian "effective reality" of phenomena, if necessary scratching off the deceptive scab of ideologies. The sense of political and social power had matured in him, so as not to let him be blinded by natural law, or at least dogmatic and a priori formulas, but to require that power be described and explained in its daily, concrete unfolding, beyond purely defining description, perhaps formally perfect but without precise empirical verification. Then, his discovery of how much irrationality human beings are capable of, and how action in society needs symbols and myths even when recourse is made to the cult of reason, is important. Whatever the personal and class prejudices of the time through which Pareto thought and wrote, his contribution to the social sciences remains today undiminished, still problematically alive and in many aspects provocative.

NOTES

1. See Maffeo Pantaleoni, "In occasione della morte di Pareto riflessioni," in *Giornale degli Economisti*, January–February 1924.

2. See, especially, V. Pareto, *Lettere ai Peruzzi, 1872–1900*, 2 vols., ed. Tomaso Giacalone-Monaco, Roma: Edizion, 1968.

3. See *Alcune lettere di Vilfredo Pareto*, publ. and ed. A. Antonucci, Roma: P. Maglione, 1938, pp. 18–20. As regards Pareto's intellectual and political development, see Dino Fiorot, *Il realismo politico di Vilfredo Pareto*, Milan: Comunità, 1969, especially the introduction, "La formazione politica e sociologica di Pareto," pp. 9–69. I comment on Fiorot's general interpretation later on. It is scarcely necessary to draw attention to G. H. Bousquet's work, especially *Pareto: le savant et l'homme*, Lausanne: Payot, 1960, and Giovanni Busino's work, especially his most informative introduction to the *Scritti sociologici di V. Pareto*, Torino: UTET, 1966, pp. 11–122.

4. See M. Pantaleoni, "In occasione della morte."

5. See Busino, "*Scritti sociologici*," pp. 11–12: ". . . the Italian contribution to the understanding of a varied and complex system of thought . . . is almost nonexistent." However, this is also true as regards scholars on the international level. It is strange to have to remark how Pareto returned to Europe, especially in Italy, bounced back from the United States, where from 1936 Talcott Parsons devoted long and hermeneutically acute attention to him (see the first volume of *The Structure of Social Action*, New York: Free Press, 1968).

6. Cf. G. La Ferla, *Vilfredo Pareto filosofo volteriano*, Firenze: La Nuova Italia, 1955.

7. See N. Bobbio's introduction to Pareto's *Trattato di sociologia generale*, 2 vols., Milano: Comunità, 1964, pp. xiii–xxxviii. (An accessible, abridged version in English of Pareto's huge work is available as V. Pareto, *Compendium of General Sociology*, ed. E. Abbot, Minneapolis: Univ. of Minnesota Press, 1979; see also, inter alia, the selections in V. Pareto, *Sociological Writings*, trans. by D. Mirfin, Totowa, N.J.: Rowman & Littlefield, repr. ed., 1976.)

8. Bobbio, introduction, p. xxxviii.

9. Cf. Fiorot, *Il realismo politico*.

10. Fiorot, *Il realismo politico*, p. 184.

11. Cf. my *Trattato di sociologia*, Torino: UTET 1968, p. 211.

12. Cf. Fiorot, *Il realismo politico*, p. 186.

12

✢

Thorstein Veblen: Radical Critic of Business Culture

It does not surprise us that Thorstein Veblen is not well known in Europe, and even less understood. Pierre Bourdieu, for instance, who uses extensively some of Veblen's basic concepts in his major work *Distinction*, an essay on the social matrix of aesthetic values, never quotes or cites him. The same is true for Italy.[1] When the Italian translation of *The Theory of the Leisure Class* appeared at the beginning of 1949,[2] the leading Italian philosopher and historian Benedetto Croce—the man whom Antonio Gramsci had labeled an "intellectual pope"—wrote a devastating critique of it.[3] In this article, Croce, the best-known spokesman of Hegelian neoidealism, charges Veblen with the "most complete obtrusiveness as regards the understanding of historical phenomena." Following that review, a broad and articulate debate ensued among scholars of widely different ideological allegiances, ranging from neoidealists to orthodox Marxists to socially minded theorists. As Veblen's translator, I participated in that debate with two essays.[4] It seems obvious, especially after the essays by Walter Benjamin on the subject, that any translation is to a degree a betrayal. Undoubtedly, the act of translating another's work requires not only close reading, but entering the mind of its author. Veblen's Italian readers, even those who thought favorably of the book, did not seem to understand the full force of Veblen's thought. For example, the bulk of Croce's criticism lies in the fact that, according to him, Veblen considered "conspicuous waste" what

I wish to thank Arthur J. Vidich for his editorial assistance and for the ideas he has discussed with me on this subject.

was actually due as a prerequisite of social respectability in a substantive way. Croce goes as far as quoting the poet Ludovico Ariosto who would regard "without honor" whoever would write the word *onore* without the *h*. However, that European intellectuals, who frequently and sometimes snobbishly disdain American thinkers, should fail to understand Veblen is perhaps excusable, if not justifiable.

What is more intriguing is that essentially the same and analogous critical misunderstandings can be found among American students of Veblen. This is surprising. After the pioneering study of the life and thought of Thorstein Veblen by Joseph Dorfman a few years after his death in 1929,[5] one could have expected a sizable amount of serious commentary and systematic study about Thorstein Veblen in the United States, especially considering the challenging view of American society and of American business practices that he expounded in his books. This is not the case. Comments are usually repetitive and secondhand. Rick Tilman and J. L. Simich[6] have compiled a comprehensive listing of works on and about Veblen. The content of this contribution confirms that many writers on Veblen have depended on secondary and even tertiary sources. No one has attempted a comprehensive interpretation based on a reading of the total corpus.

One has the impression that even in the United States Veblen's writings remain still unknown in their entirety and have not been read carefully as a complete body. What is worse, a disturbing trait seems to surface also when one reads through writers who comment on one or another part of the Veblenian corpus: amusing anecdotes and curious legends about his personality are conflated with his analyses, at the expense of a serious examination of the substance of his interpretations. Such anecdotal material includes prurient comments about his sexual life, his personal reclusiveness, his unwillingness to suffer fads, and his disregard of conventional social forms. Stressing these aspects of his character leads to a polemical trivialization conveyed in order to dismantle, without really facing them squarely and openly, his major theses, with special reference to the role of the American businessmen in politics and international affairs, credit institutions, business cycles, the relations between industrial productivity and business practices, intellectuals, and universities, to mention only a few of the topics dealt with in his books.

Criticism by innuendo and what I would call character assassination is apparent, among others, in the work by David Riesman.[7] The preface to the paperback edition in 1960 is signed by David Riesman and Staughton Lynd and admits to an emphasis on "contradictions and ambiguities" in Veblen's thought as an a priori starting point. Actually, what a dispassionate reader soon finds out in this entertaining book is that Veblen's theoretical positions and social interpretations are not judged on the basis of their ability to describe and eventually explain specific issues and situations of the American social system. Rather, there is a constant effort to relate Veblen's thinking to contemporary writers, whether Veblen's theories do or do not fit the problems they are supposed to tackle. Riesman's effort is a good illustration of how to make books through books which selectively diminish an author's ideas. Moreover, these ideas are diminished by a psychological undertone pervading Riesman's interpretation. Inevitably, given such a presupposition, Riesman's account of Veblen tends to become gossipy. The amusement is granted, but both a fair presentation and ideas are bound to suffer.

Riesman believes it is important to understand Veblen's father in order to understand the work of the son, but even here, Riesman grossly exaggerates the influence of Veblen's father on his son: "One might . . . say that Thomas Veblen's willingness to learn new farming techniques but his unwillingness to learn new linguistic ones was the model for the son's admiration for production per se, accomplished without 'waste,' 'naturally,' without the frills of cultivation or nuances of style."[8] It is surprising that such a refined analyst as Riesman would make here a confusion between new farm equipment and a new language. Remaining faithful, as it were, to the old language of one's birth has a lot to do with a recognition of one's roots and cultural identity, while acquiring new farm machinery might only be a question of not being phased out of the market. As regards the father–son relationship, contradictions seem more abundant in Riesman than in Veblen. Riesman goes so far as to state that "Veblen appears never to have exorcised his father,"[9] and yet, he cannot help remarking that Veblen praises "masterless men" throughout history. Riesman recalls and evidently enjoys an anecdote reported by R. L. Duffus, a Veblen student who lived with him for a year: "when the elder Veblen went to town on a market day and happened to meet his son in the street he did not speak to him or give any sign of recognition. I gathered that the Professor thought this interesting but not extraordinary: 'If a man had nothing to say there was no use in talking, even to his son.'"[10] Riesman makes no effort to try to understand the Norwegian immigrant milieu in America nor the expression of filial piety in the older clan structure of traditional Norway. He refuses to recognize significant cultural facts that one would expect a sociologist to use automatically in an interpretation involving the relationship between character and social structure.

The city-born Riesman is surprised and perhaps scandalized by this father–son relationship which was the norm in a rural Norwegian milieu. He seems to regard it as conclusive evidence of paternal authoritarianism against which Veblen, the "natural anarchist," should by all counts rebel. Yet, Riesman is forced to recognize that Veblen claimed that "his father had taught him more than any other man." Maybe Jean-Paul Sartre (of

The Words) would be in agreement with Riesman, and perhaps also Franz
Kafka (of the *Letter to his Father*) would not take issue with him about the
cumbersome and "heavy" role of the father, pontificating at the head of
the dining table, vis-à-vis the other family members. As far as understanding Veblen is concerned, Riesman's psychological interpretation is
contradictory and unconvincing, not to mention that it misleads him into
his own work. Riesman is talking more about his relationship with his
own father than that of Veblen with his. In a 1989 profile written about
Riesman in the Harvard Alumni Magazine called *Harvard*, Riesman
speaks of a father who did not think him worthy, who had expectations
for him which he could not fulfill and implies that his career was a com-
pensation for that relationship.

For Riesman, Veblen was essentially a marginal man, a man who had
special difficulties in establishing any sort of contact with his fellowmen
or his milieu, his colleagues and his readers. He sees in Veblen's very writing style, which is sardonic, allusive, often indirect, and ironical, nothing
but a reflection of his presumed inability to communicate: "In print as in
person, he appears not to have felt that he had an audience, that he could
communicate; his books and even his long articles, taken as a whole, con-
vey an obsessive quality, as of a man who fears he will not be heard. . . .
It goes without saying that communication is a two-way affair, and the
other side of Veblen's inability to make himself heard was his inability to
listen to the meaning of many intellectual attitudes which might have
proved provocative to him. Thus, the narrow circle of his friends is
matched by the narrow circle of his citations."[11]

This interpretation borders on the scandalous. Any reader of Veblen's
analyses of utilitarianism, pragmatism, Marxism, and so on will not only
find citations, but learn that Veblen had read deeply in them and took the
trouble to understand them in their own terms. One should note also that
the first chapter of *The Instinct of Workmanship* is fully annotated with reference to all major psychologists of the period. The idea never even enters
Riesman's mind that maybe Veblen kept to himself because he did not
share that kind of gregarious feeling that prevails in so many conformist
institutional environments. From a substantive point of view, what Riesman perceived as a pathological and mostly self-imposed marginality
might simply indicate that Veblen kept his distance in order to be critical.
He had refused to join the herd of independent academic minds because
they were his subject matter. But I feel that the shrewd psychologization,
and through it the intellectual debasing of Veblen by Riesman, reaches its
climax when he brings up the anecdote of Veblen tearing to pieces his log
cabin in California. According to Riesman, this would be a clear evidence
of aggressive behavior due to the inhibitions of a pathologically timid person that at a certain point simply and quite unreasonably "explodes."

This is even more preposterous than reducing the whole of Veblen's work to a "dialogue between his father and mother." No effort to evaluate the "objective situation" is made or at least attempted. Had Riesman done his homework, he might also have mentioned that at the time of the log cabin incident Veblen decided then and there to write perhaps his greatest book, *Absentee Ownership*.

There are other failures and weaknesses in Riesman's interpretation which are worth mentioning because they are revealing of some wide-spread American cultural propensities. I would not dwell on the depressing confusion between Darwin and Hegel—a confusion that Veblen, perceptive student of both, and of Marx—manages never to fall into. "Despite his admiration for Darwin," Riesman writes, "Veblen distrusted Hegel's developmental logic."[12] In fact, one should read: Because he admired Darwin, he had to distrust Hegel's dialectical impatience. Such clever academic jousting on Riesman's part could be examined in more detail, but a complete and serious examination of the points adumbrated by this interpretive style would take us too far. In particular, one would have to spell out in detail the qualitative difference, if not the contradictory *coupure*, between an evolutionary and a dialectical approach.

A mention, however, should be made of the problem posed by technology. According to Riesman, Veblen is essentially a technocrat, a "true believer" in the machine and in what he called the "machine discipline," obviously destined to shape human bents and propensities, habits of mind and practical behavioral patterns. Undoubtedly, technology is not conceived the same way by Marx and Veblen. But an unbiased reading of Marx should make it clear that the prime mover of social process is, in his judgment, to be seen in terms of "social relationships," based on a given (technical) mode of production. This Marxian concept of *soziale Verhält-nisse* prevails upon all the rest. In Veblen, quite to the contrary, the perspective is always strictly individualistic. In this respect, Veblen appears to be more "technologically minded," as it were, than Marx. This is recognized by Riesman, who fails, however, to underline that Veblen never falls victim of the myth of class consciousness, not even when he talks of an "engineers' society," as being the "chosen instrument" to bring about the socialist revolution. Does this make Veblen a technocrat? Riesman seems quite certain that Veblen was in fact a technocrat. "[T]hat the worker was brutalized by the machine," he writes, "Veblen combatted as the one-eyed projection of men familiar only with the animistic thinking, and hence unable to conceive of a mechanistic kind of intelligence."[13] Misunderstanding Veblen's conception of animistic thinking, Riesman also fails to see the full import of what he understands by the discipline of the machine. Not only does the machine set the terms of work for the worker, but the machine gives its character to the society as a whole.

Riesman's analysis of the machine, machine industry, and technology is tainted with prejudice. His analysis assumes that Veblen had little knowledge of factories and factory life. But then he is faced with an important question mark: where did Veblen get his "sympathy," if not his love affair, for machines? Riesman admits that such an attitude is rare among intellectuals. In a sense, he seems to agree with C. P. Snow's views about "the two cultures and the scientific revolution." In other words, he sees a profound, perhaps insurmountable dichotomy between the humanistic, literary, and philosophical culture and the culture grounded on a mathematical, matter-of-fact, and "scientific" outlook. It is well known that such a strict separation has no meaning in any actual scientific research. Every research at the critical level happens to be in need of both imagination, since it starts within a context of discovery, and empirical testing, that is, a methodical application of research techniques which fall within the scope of the context of validation. It is clear that scholars cannot be grossly divided into two groups; for example, those who know Shakespeare by heart and those who are well versed with the second law of thermodynamics. But in Riesman, once again, the explanation of the strange "sympathy" of Veblen for machines is looked for and supposedly found in purely psychological terms: "I have already noted that his father was unique among his group of Norwegian immigrants in mechanizing his farm operations. It is quite conceivable that this Thomas Veblen sat for the portrait which Thorstein Veblen, years later, drew of the engineer. Moreover, Veblen was a farm boy who didn't like farming, or doing by hand anything a machine could be invented to do, was almost completely free of the rural yearning or nostalgia of many enemies of the industrial revolution."[14] It is amazing that Riesman does not point out in this respect how discriminating the "sympathy" or even the acceptance of the industrial revolution on the part of Veblen was: Veblen certainly accepted technical innovation and industrial progress, but this does not mean that he would accept industrialism en bloc. In fact, one of his major contributions to the analysis of contemporary industrial society must be seen in his keen distinction between the captains of industry and the captains of business, the productive manager and the speculator, the *brasseur d'affaires*. And, in fact, if Riesman had read *Absentee Ownership*, he would have learned that Veblen's portrait of the businessman-speculator-confidence man has, according to Veblen, its origins in the small-town land and grain speculator—that same small town of Veblen's origin, where the immigrant farmer was always exploited by the town-based businessman who played on the farmers' greed for more land.

What Riesman seems to grant to Veblen's insight is the influence of technically advanced work upon the attitudes of workers. Here there is a definite advance with respect to Marx and other socialist thinkers who felt that workers, with the collapse of capitalism had "nothing to lose but their chains," to use the Marxian and Engelsian phrase in the *Manifesto* of 1848. Veblen, who was never fooled by any myth of class solidarity and special "mission" of the proletariat, knew that workers off the job would risk not only their income, and therefore their means of subsistence, but their skill as well. They would lose, with "their chains," the positive influence of the "machine discipline" also. But when Riesman examines the theory of the instinct of workmanship, he does not seem capable of discerning the true contribution by Veblen, although this contribution is certainly buried under the verbiage of the anthropological and biological jargon in the first chapter of the book where Veblen essentially denies the utility of the concept of instinct, so fashionable then among many psychologists and philosophers. Perhaps Riesman deserves some excuse in this connection: at the beginning of *The Instinct of Workmanship* Veblen devotes nearly forty pages to develop what sounds like a biological theory of instincts, but at the same time he is almost compulsively repeating that "instincts" do not develop in any deterministic way, that they are usually mixed and "contaminated," as it were, and—most important of all—that they are historically conditioned ("in all their working, the human instincts are . . . incessantly subject to mutual 'contamination'").[15] "Parental bent" and "instinct of workmanship" are conceived by Veblen as belonging to human beings as common dispositions or "hereditary spiritual traits." He writes: "Chief among those instinctive dispositions that conduce directly to the well being of the race, and therefore to its biological success, is perhaps the instinctive bias here spoken of as the sense of workmanship. The only other instinctive factor of human nature that could with any likelihood dispute this primacy would be the parental bent. Indeed, the two have much in common."[16]

The question of "instincts" and of their conceptual definition is a difficult one in Veblen. "In making use of the expression 'instinct of workmanship' or 'sense of workmanship,'" Veblen writes, "is not here intended to assume or to argue that the proclivity so designated is in the psychological respect a simple and irreducible element; still less, of course, is there *any intention to allege that it is to be traced back in the physiological respect to some one isolable tropismatic sensibility or some enzymatic or visceral stimulus.*"[17]

The text seems sufficiently clear, and yet, it is extraordinary that such a sophisticated analyst as Riesman would not see what is hidden behind the word "instinct". The very fact that W. Ogburn's concept of "cultural lag" has been evoked should have indicated that the meaning of the term is not found in a biological or purely physiological sense. Moreover, Veblen expounds time and again the theme of "contamination" among different instincts or "instinctual drives." He constantly relates the instincts not so much to "hereditary traits" in the biological sense—a phrase that he occasionally uses—but rather to social environment and cultural tradition. This is the underlying reason why he is entitled to write about "contamination of instincts." His usage of the word is anthropological rather than biological. Hence, instincts in Veblen refer to institutions which are man-made; that is, instincts are historical; they are not fixed traits, given once and for all; they can change in accordance with a changing institutional environment and with a changing set of functional prerequisites.

This is perhaps not the place to go deep into an examination of Riesman's strictures on Veblen's ideas concerning the conduct of American universities by businessmen. It is hardly to be expected that the complacent author of *Variety and Constraint in American Education*,[18] and the felicitous inventor of the formula "the academic procession" could fully understand the tension between business logic and scientific research as described by Veblen who, as is well known, regarded his considerations about the Higher Learning in America as a "study in total depravity." All of Riesman's work on higher education in America fails to make use of Veblen's central discoveries about the modern university (for example, its bureaucratization, its resort to public relations, the corruption of its administrators, and its close association with the business community).

According to the interpretation by Riesman, the essence of Veblen's critical spirit must be attributed to the fact that he is alienated, that he is a typical marginal man. But, at the same time, Riesman sees in Veblen the peasant, the boy that grew up on a farm, a "giant out of the earth." This sounds contradictory. The peasant is self-assured, well rooted in his soil. What Riesman does not seem to understand is that Veblen is simply trying to look at society from a certain distance in order to be able to look at it with a dry eye. Finally, however, again in a blatant contradiction with his overall psychological dilution of Veblen's insights and analyses, Riesman is forced to acknowledge his ability to forecast the advent of Nazism in Germany and to interpret correctly, beyond the gold and glitz of the roaring twenties, the profound need for a reordering of the American social and economic landscape. One can easily understand why Riesman, a coherent conservative with liberal overtones, fails to question himself seriously as regards the weight and scope of Veblen's analysis of American society. He chooses to consider such analysis as a projection of Veblen's "inner drives." In this way, he sees that analysis as the mere psychotic expression of Veblen's existential *défaillances* vis-à-vis the requirements for making a career for oneself in contemporary industrial society.

Strangely enough, at the opposite pole of Riesman's political and ideological spectrum, C. Wright Mills also falls below an acceptable critical level when dealing with the general position of Veblen. The contribution of Thorstein Veblen to social science can be "diminished," if not altogether wiped out, in a variety of ways. Usually, conservative commentators, from his contemporary academic colleagues to Robert Heilbroner, reduce his role and thought through appropriately delivered trivial anecdotes and gossip. C. Wright Mills is original in this respect. He tends to emphasize literary form, or style, at the expense of specific content. He writes: "All the assertions get disproved sooner or later; and so we find the world full of magnificent debris of artistic forms, with the matter-of-fact credibility gone clean out of them, but the form still splendid."[19] Are we then to believe that Veblen's analyses are beautifully written, and therefore highly enjoyable, while their content no longer holds any meaning? Mills acknowledges that Veblen was a great social thinker, and not a mere social technician, that in fact he was a professional antispecialist: "A social thinker in the grand tradition , for he tried to do what Hegel and Comte and Marx and Spencer and Weber—each in his own way—had tried to do."[20] Yet, quite astonishingly, Mills feels that Veblen was a "profoundly conservative critic of America." This is a surprising statement, considering that Veblen suggested doing away with the stock market, eliminating the businessmen/boards of trustees of universities, and replacing businessmen and bankers with engineers.

A couple of paragraphs earlier, Mills had stated that "Veblen was a sort of intellectual wobbly."[21] And a little earlier still, that, far from wobbling, Veblen was "a sure-footed old man."[22] It is an eye-catching, though disturbing, mixture of contradictions. The fact is that Mills, like many other sympathetic commentators—notably Max Lerner—cannot see the political reasoning of Veblen behind the anthropological pyrotechnics that he enjoyed so much. On the other hand, just like Max Weber when he talked about *Wertfreiheit*, or "value-freedom," Veblen seems at times prevented by a sense of shame from making his own commitments explicit. He pretends to be neutral, although his criticism can be, and actually is, devastating. It is no wonder that the political element and commitment of Veblen, mostly indirect and rarely explicit, totally escapes generous but perhaps fast readers such as Mills, whose heart is in the right place but whose attention to nuances does not seem to be adequate. Mills was more the hustler than serious student of Veblen.

According to Mills, Veblen is basically a technocrat, only one of Mills's major misunderstandings. The militant, boisterous Texan simply could not follow the elaborate intricacies and the allusive nature of a Veblenian text. Veblen, in Mills's opinion, is a technocrat because "he wholeheartedly accepted one of the few un-ambiguous, all-American values: the value of efficiency, of utility, of pragmatic simplicity."[23] In other words, Veblen was criticizing America for not being American enough. But, what about the Veblen who theorizes, and practices up to a point, sabotage? Mills would perhaps reply that, in terms of scientific acquisitions, the value of *The Theory of the Leisure Class*, if any, is at most a retrospective one. That way of life is over; that kind of leisure class does not make history, if it ever did. The author of *The Power Elite* finds, understandably enough, the Veblenian leisure class not sufficiently muscular nor prone to make deals in smoke-filled rooms, more dedicated to sports and conspicuous waste than to planning the future for mankind. In the opinion of Mills, the analysis of Veblen does not have any importance nor impact on present-day society, that is to say, in a society in which the three top layers—the social, the economic, and the military—seem to coalesce and to be driven by a powerful converging urge: they play together, they go to school together, they work together, they marry together. They tend to think the same way and to decide things the same way, to like and dislike the same things. But Veblen's analysis cuts deeper than Mills's. When we consider the contemporary crises of credit institutions, not to mention the "predators' ball" of the takeovers during the Reagan years, and the incredible farm foreclosures of the so-called "affluent society," we can easily see that the Paretian concept of *élite* is perhaps too psychological in tone and ambiguous in substance to carry the burden of a research centering, as it should, on impoverished farm families, junk bonds, and the new robber barons of Reaganomics. Mills did not bother to read Veblen from the point of view of his theory of the State which is analyzed wholly within the framework of the community of businessmen in and out of government. It is true that *The Theory of the Leisure Class*, as Mathew Josephson[24] rightly observes, is a study of the new post–Civil War upper class of captains of business, but Veblen's analysis of the businessman as the archetype of the American character is not limited to that book. Veblen may not have had an opportunity to observe the rise of the managerial class, but he understood quite well that the managers had not supplanted the business leaders of the country.

Perhaps, more than an intellectual wobbly, Veblen should be regarded as the last "muckraker." But Veblen could be considered only an "honorary" muckraker. In other words, Veblen, who was writing in the era of muckraking, as symbolized by Lincoln Steffens, might be considered not a muckraker in the traditional sense, but the one critic who transcended the superficial moralizing of the muckraking journalists. In this sense, Veblen might be regarded rightly as the deep-digging muckraker of American hypocrisy, illusionism, and fraud, especially keeping in mind his relentless battle against the captains of business, exclusively eager to make their million at the expense of everyone else. What divides Veblen from the moralistic muckrakers of the turn of the century was their stance of indignation at social injustice, financial greed, and political corruption. For this reason, the placement of Veblen in the ranks of the muckrakers, as has been eloquently advocated by George P. Rawick and Irving Louis Horowitz, is neither well grounded nor acceptable. Perhaps one could apply this label to C. Wright Mills who, as is evident from a reading of his book, *The Marxists*,[25] never quite understood Marx, or Veblen for that matter, and to the end confused the Hegelian concept of dialectics with the scholastic *ars disserendi*. Veblen's understanding of Marx remains to this day the definitive critical analysis of his system. Those who have thought of Veblen as a muckraker have failed, like Mills, to fully understand Veblen's critique of Marx. That critique, developed in essays written before 1900, proves Veblen to have a deep understanding not only of economics but also of philosophy, including Hegelianism. As I have noted in an article mentioned above,[26] Veblen knew Marx in depth and was able to uncover serious aporias in the Marxian theoretical construction. Some of his critical points are still relevant today, especially after the collapse of "real socialism" in Eastern Europe and in the Soviet Union.

Notably in "Some Neglected Points in the Theory of Socialism" and "The Socialist Economics of Karl Marx and His Followers,"[27] it is impressive how Veblen, contrary to most commentators of his day, is aware of the many-sided nature of Marxism as a system. Moreover, Veblen knows that a piecemeal criticism of Marxism, both favorable and unfavorable, is bound to be meaningless because it would necessarily fall short of a headlong confrontation with Marx's basic logical structure, that is, with the movement of Hegelian dialectic.[28] But where Lenin is indirect, Veblen is explicit: "Except as a whole and except in the light of its postulates and aims, the Marxian system is not only not tenable, but it is not even intelligible. A discussion of a given isolated feature of the system (such as the theory of value) from the point of view of classical economics (such as that offered by Böhm-Bawerk) is as futile as a discussion of solids in terms of two dimensions."[29] Even more specifically Veblen understands, at the turn of the century (!), what has not yet been understood today, even among official Marxists, that everything is already in the first volume of *Capital* and that the other two volumes, edited by Friedrich Engels, "add nothing essential."[30] Hardline Marxists have had difficulties coping with the Veblenian critique, and for the most part have had recourse to disputing Veblen's credentials rather than his argument. Paul A. Baran, dealing with *The Theory of the Leisure Class*, is satisfied to regard Veblen as a "bourgeois theorist" and as a "bourgeois historian." "Like other bourgeois theorists," Baran writes, "Veblen has recourse to invoking *dei ex machina* as an ultimate means of interpretation. And again, as in the case of most bourgeois historians, Veblen's wisdoms of last resort are always of a biological or psychological nature, have always something to do with 'basic' racial characteristics of men or with the no less 'fundamental' structure of their motivations . . . Veblen never relinquishes his biological-psychological apparatus."[31] Baran's collaborator, Paul M.

Sweezy, on the other hand, considers Veblen simply as "a theorist who dealt almost wholly in generalities and hardly ever introduced a statistic into his writings."[32] Yet Sweezy acknowledges that "Veblen's general diagnosis of "the state of the nation" is . . . astonishingly accurate and if anything more relevant to 1957 than to 1904 or 1923."[33] One might add that it is perhaps even more relevant today. What seems to escape these peculiarly American (because they are still grounded in a form of social moralism) left-wing commentators is that for Veblen, as well as for Marx, men and women are a source of energy, animals manifesting themselves through initiatives and efforts, producing and reproducing themselves. For Marx, this productive energy creates a surplus which is "stolen" by the capitalists and reinvested by them to their own exclusive advantage. It is evident that Marx's perspective is still basically "rational," so much so that "the romantic (Marxian) sequence of theory is essentially an intellectual sequence, and it is therefore of a teleological character."[34] For Veblen, on the contrary, there is no assurance that the surplus will be used rationally by human beings. In this respect Veblen is closer to Vilfredo Pareto than to Marx. He sees the "psychic income" and, without the benefit of a firsthand knowledge of Freud, the subliminal motivations that go with irrational "conspicuous waste" and the social respectability that accrues from it. In this sense not only does Veblen go beyond Marx but his analysis holds true today as it did then. The coherent critique of economic hedonism and of the supposedly highly rational *homo economicus* on the part of Veblen gives him an insight into the unanticipated consequences of irrational behavioral patterns that allows Veblen to anticipate with impressive precision the *Dialectic of Enlightenment* by Max Horkheimer and Theodor Adorno and in general the criticism of the illusory capitalist rationality which remains the backbone of the Frankfurt School. It should be enough to mention how Veblen sees the possibility that the sportsmanlike propensities of the masses, whose interest and allegiance are captured by mass sports events, could be used and politically exploited by a shrewd political dictator, well versed in the fine art of propaganda. It is difficult not to think of the 1936 Olympic Games in Berlin and of their deft use by Hitler and Goebbels. The critical strictures of Adorno with regard to the general position of Veblen, presented as a crude technocrat and a hater of culture as such, cannot blur the fact that, long before the Frankfurt School, Veblen pointed out some definite characteristics of mass society and mass culture as well as the crisis of nineteenth-century values.

Among American commentators, even among the most favorably inclined, Veblen remains, however, a pure and simple technocrat. The text on which this definition of Veblen's thinking is based, by some carried to the point of making it a mere predecessor of the "theories" expounded in 1932 by Howard Scott, is *The Engineers and the Price System*. But even in this book for Veblen, of all the factors making for waste, perhaps the most important was "salesmanship." In his perspective, this factor went well beyond that of the technical restriction of output to emphasize its grounding in psychological manipulation with a greater rigor than even Adorno or Horkheimer ever achieved. Economists have not yet read Veblen's economics as one that contains a theory of waste; the attribution of waste to unproductive labor is refuted over and over again.

Veblen cannot be reduced nor confined within the framework of the technocratic movement of the early twenties, no matter how some commentators have so categorized him. From the point of view of both psychological and economic theory, Veblen goes beyond and deeper than that technocratic reasoning, holding that all political and social problems of the age could be solved in purely technical and organizational engineering. This is what I have called the "organizational myth,"[35] that is, the belief that suggests the possibility of forgetting about the political problem of power and resource allocation through a purely technical, a-political approach. Veblen is far from such a position. Partly concealed by his indirect and at times esoteric style, Veblen is essentially a political thinker, dealing with the central issues of social fairness and power. The political *animus* of Veblen's thought has been explored at length by Rick Tilman,[36] but the technocratic bent is entertained even among some neo-Veblenians. As it has been aptly remarked, "the metaphysics of this (instinct of workmanship) have not been acceptable to neo-Veblenians, and their writings do not depend on this proposition. A few of them do, however, use a variant form of mechanistic determinism—one that may be said to have a technocratic twist."[37] It remains to be satisfactorily explained how Veblen, who had exploded conclusively the fallacy of hedonism, that is, the rational model of *homo economicus* of the classical political economists and who had shown the residual utilitarian elements, even in Marx, could be mistaken for a technocrat. It is true that economists never seemed to take Veblen seriously. It could be noted that Joseph A. Schumpeter, for example, in his *History of Economic Analysis* does not treat either Veblen or Weber in the full dimensions they deserve and also that he borrows heavily from both of them whom he most surely read with great care. Schumpeter refers to Veblen as "candid" or, at most, as a "depredation theory ancestor" or, and this seems to be a major concession, as a "critic of marginal utility."[38] It is easy to maintain that "the psychological theories of the neo-Veblenians dispose them to espouse many causes that Veblen himself would have considered futile."[39] This is naturally even more true for non-Veblenians among psychologists, and more so among the economists. The conception of Veblen's thought as a variant, no matter how important, of technocracy is a seriously limiting conception that amounts to a major misunderstanding of Veblen's theoretical and political position.

The fact that Veblen never, or rarely, wrote about issues which were explicitly political has to do with the spirit of the time and its peculiar characteristics. The simple reason is that Veblen did not have to write explicitly about politics to be a political writer. Before the advent of the New Deal it was sufficient to write about the businessman. He was the hero of the American success story; he was both an economic force and a political leader. Government action was reduced to a minimum. Government initiatives did not exist. Only after the New Deal and with the coming into power of Franklin D. Roosevelt did the government, that is, the explicitly political dimension, become apparent. At that point, and actually a few years before, Veblen's political stand was made evident through his editorials in *The Dial* and *The Freeman*. In these articles one finds in Veblen a militant political writer who would be extremely difficult to accommodate within the framework of a technically addicted technocrat. From this vantage point, his *The Engineers and the Price System* acquires a new light and a totally different dimension. What sounds technocratic is actually the preparation for a radically new policy, the policy of an "engineers' soviet," thinking and acting according to rational criteria against the dead hand of vested interests and animistic, irrational habits of mind.

It is disturbing that again, even in a sympathetic writer like John Kenneth Galbraith (as he writes in his introduction to a 1973 edition of *The Theory of the Leisure Class*), this aspect is not properly understood. Galbraith rightly remarks that Veblen was not a social reformer in the traditional sense. In other words, he did not conceive history as endowed with automatic organizational abilities as the Hegelians, right and left, would have it. According to Galbriath, Veblen was not favorable to the proletariat nor to the poor nor to the oppressed. But, how does he know? He was, in Galbraith's opinion, not a revolutionary, but a man full of hostility. Here again, a psychological interpretation victimizes Veblen. Galbraith is definitely wrong in this respect. Veblen was irked by wastefulness, stupidity, the businessman as a conman (advertising) and anything that was not matter-of-fact and rational. His matter-of-factness and rationality saw irrationality everywhere. The hostility of Veblen, contrary to what Riesman thought, is not due, according to Galbraith, to resentment for his own sufferings during his childhood, but to contempt and derision: contempt against the city storekeepers, the saloon owners, the salesmen and importers of wheat, and so on. But it seems that even the word "contempt" misses the mark because it is too strong. Veblen mocked the big businessman for his misplaced self-confidence. He chided the academic administrators for their self-appointed importance. He ridiculed the small businessman for his pettiness—cheating people out of pennies. Veblen's hero is the common man, a vague term, never defined, but probably referring to the working stiffs, the people who actually produce something useful, not only material goods, but ideas, inventions, and anything socially useful—to the betterment of the community.

Not only in America but almost everywhere, commentators have complained about Veblen's lack of an articulate political awareness as well as, more specifically, of a theory of the State. Yet, a whole chapter on Imperial Germany and the industrial revolution is entitled "The Dynastic State." Would it be possible to be more explicit than this about the "political dimension"? More precisely, the view of Thorstein Veblen as an a-political technocrat can only be sustained if one overlooks his articles and essays first published in *The Dial* and *The Freedom*. I would mention in particular, "Bolshevism is a Menace—To Whom?"[40] and "Bolshevism and the Vested Interests in America"[41] and "Dementia Praecox."[42] The first two articles deal with issues of general political and economic theory while the third one tackles a problem of international politics. Their political relevance is self-evident. However, not even John P. Diggins, by far the most penetrating interpreter of Veblen seems to understand the political substance and impact of Veblen's thinking.[43]

Undoubtedly, Veblen was the first writer to raise the problem of technocracy and of "managerial revolution" in America, long before James Burnham, Alvin W. Gouldner, and John Kenneth Galbraith, among others. It is interesting to note that none of these authors ever acknowledged his debt to Veblen, who clearly and independently went beyond any notion of a politically netutral "technostructure" or "totally administered society." In contrast to Daniel Lerner's view, for Veblen economics and politics were not separable. When Veblen separated them, he did so for the essentially analytical purpose of scientific exploration. Lerner writes: "Veblen found it unnecessary to do much in the way of the explicit formulation of a theory of politics. His ideas about political power are implicit in his ideas about social power and in his whole theory of how institutions are rooted in men's habits. . . . His analysis of the State might have been a fuller one if he had not approached political power wholly by way of economic power and its psychological bolstering."[44] However, it is to Lerner's credit that he recognizes the positive features of Veblen's supposed limitations. Lerner rightly maintains that Veblen anticipated both Arnold Toynbee and Oswald Spengler by focusing his research on the analysis of civilizations taken as more or less coherent wholes rather than on the nation-state which he considers basically doomed with its frontiers easily bypassed by technology, science, and the world market with the multinational companies as its dominating actors. At the same time, it is important to note that Veblen was not a victim of any petty-minded "discipline patriotism," as he would move freely, almost nonchalantly, from discipline to discipline in a general perspective which, more than interdisciplinary, could be more appropriately labeled as "post-disciplinary."

This may help to explain why American academics have not provided us with comprehensive exegetical works on Veblen's thought comparable to those that have been done, for example, on Weber or Marx.

On the one hand, academic specialization—and its increasing prevalence these days—makes it difficult for his critics and admirers to gain a full grasp of the scope of his work. On the other, Veblen's use of the English language is both imaginative and nontechnical—therefore unfamiliar to most of his academic readers. Veblen's usage comes close to being a form of poetry—that is, sharpness of images, use of metaphor, preciseness in choice of vocabulary, and, above all, inventiveness of expression that does not lend itself to simple slogans as does the language of Freud or Marx. The fact is that, to this day, the great majority of American critics treat Veblen very selectively. They tend to forget that *The Theory of the Leisure Class* is not his most important book. His major contribuiton to social theory, endowed with an extraordinary predictive value, is his penetrating analysis of capitalism in the United States, Germany, and Japan. These studies remain relevant today. It is still not understood that technology and anthropology for Veblen were used as foils to highlight the irrationality of Western civilization and capitalism, reversing the thrust of the anthropologists who highlighted the irrationality of the world of primitives to which Veblen gave the benefit of rationality.

In summary, almost nobody seems to feel that Veblen is important enough to deal with his work as a whole. They are satisfied with ad hoc references and superficial readings in the same vein as the European sociologist Ralf Dahrendorf, who writes in his book *Freedom in Transition* that the "otherwise irascible and peculiar critic of America, Veblen, had something good to say about American capitalism." This most recent monumental misunderstanding is indicative of the long and difficult road that, on both sides of the Atlantic, must still be traveled to give justice to Thorstein Veblen's examination of Western civilization.

NOTES

1. See Rick Tilman and Andrea Fontana, "Italian Debate and Dialogue on Th. Veblen," in *American Journal of Economics and Sociology*, vol. 44, n. 1, January 1985, pp. 81–94.

2. *La teoria della classe agiata*, Torino: Einaudi, 1949.

3. See B. Croce, "La teoria della classe agiata," in *Corriere della Sera*, 15 January 1949.

4. See "La sociologia di Thorstein Veblen," in *Rivista di Filosofia*, vol. 41, n. 4, 1950, pp. 402–19; "Un critico americano di Marx," in *Rivista di Filosofia*, vol. 42, n. 2, 1951, pp. 154–63; and "Sulla fortuna del Veblen," in *Critica Economica*, vol. 4, n. 3, 1949, pp. 98–100 (selections from this controversy have been translated into

English in "The Reception of Veblen's *The Theory of the Leisure Class* in Italy: A Controversial Exchange," *International Journal of Politics, Culture and Society*, vol. 13, n. 2, Winter 1999, pp. 333–46.

5. See J. Dorfman, *Thorstein Veblen and His America*, New York: Viking Press, 1935.

6. See "On the Use and Abuse of Thorstein Veblen in Contemporary American Sociology," *American Journal of Economics and Sociology*, October 1983, pp. 417–28.

7. Published in 1953 by Scribner's, that text and the preface to the 1960 paperback edition are in David Riesman, *Thorstein Veblen: A Critical Interpretation*, New York: Seabury Press, 1975.

8. Riesman, *Thorstein Veblen*, p. 6.

9. Riesman, *Thorstein Veblen*, p. 8.

10. R. L. Duffus, *The Innocents at Cedro*, New York: Macmillan, 1944, p. 59.

11. Riesman, *Thorstein Veblen*, pp. 37–38.

12. Riesman, *Thorstein Veblen*, p. ix.

13. Riesman, *Thorstein Veblen*, p. 85.

14. Riesman, *Thorstein Veblen*.

15. Veblen, *The Instinct of Workmanship*, New York: Macmillan, 1914, p. 40.

16. Veblen, *The Instinct of Workmanship*, p. 25.

17. Veblen, *The Instinct of Workmanship*, p. 27 (my emphasis).

18. D. Riesman, *Variety and Constraint in American Education*, New York: Anchor Books, 1960.

19. See C. Wright Mills's 1953 introduction to Thorstein Veblen, *The Theory of the Leisure Class*, New Brunswick, N.J.: Transaction Publishers, c.1992, p. vi.

20. Mills, 1953 introduction, p. x.

21. Mills, 1953 introduction, p. ix.

22. Mills, 1953 introduction, p. viii.

23. Mills, 1953 introduction, p. xi.

24. M. Josephson, *The Robber Barons*, New York: Harcourt, Brace & World, 1962.

25. C. Wright Mills, *The Marxists*, New York: Dell Publishing, 1962.

26. See "Un critico americano di Marx," note 4 above.

27. Reproduced in *The Place of Science in Modern Civilization and Other Essays*, New York: Russell and Russell, 1961, pp. 387–456.

28. In this respect, there is an interesting confirmation of Veblen's interpretation in Lenin, *Cahiers sur la dialectique de Hegel*, trans. by H. Lefebvre and N. Guteman, Paris: Gallimard, 1967, p. 175: "Aphorisme. On ne peut comprendre le *Capital* de Marx et en particulier son premier chapitre sans avoir étudié et compris toute la *Logique* de Hegel. Donc, pas un marxiste n'a compris Marx un demi-siècle après lui."

29. Veblen, *The Place of Science*, p. 410.

30. Veblen, *The Place of Science*, p. 428.

31. See P. A. Baran, "The Theory of the Leisure Class," *Monthly Review*, vol. 9, nn. 3–4, July–August 1957, pp. 85–86.

32. See P. M. Sweezy, "The Theory of Business Enterprise and Absentee Ownership," *Monthly Review*, vol. 9, nn. 3–4, July–August 1957, p. 106.

33. Sweezy, "The Theory of Business Enterprise," p. 107.

34. Veblen, *The Place of Science*, p. 436.

35. See my *Il dilemma dei sindacati americani*, Milano: Comunità, 1954.

36. See his "Thorstein Veblen and the New Deal: A Reappraisal," *The Historian*, February 1988, pp. 22–39; "John Dewey's Liberalism versus Thorstein Veblen's Radicalism: A Reappraisal of the Unity of Progressive Social Thought," *Journal of Economic Issues*, September 1984, pp. 745–69.

37. See John S. Gambs, *Beyond Supply and Demand—A Reappraisal of Institutional Economics*, New York: Columbia Univ. Press, 1946, p. 38.

38. See J. A. Schumpeter, *History of Econmic Analysis*, New York: Oxford Univ. Press, 1954, pp. 892, 896, 911.

39. See John S. Gambs, *Beyond Supply and Demand*, p. 40.

40. *The Dial*, 22 February 1919.

41. *The Dial*, 4 October 1919.

42. *The Freeman*, 21 June 1922.

43. See especially John P. Diggins, *The Bard of Savagery: Thorstein Veblen and Modern Social Theory*, New York: Seabury Press, 1978.

44. See D. Lerner, "Introduction" to *The Portable Veblen*, New York: Viking Press, 1948, pp. 27–28.

+ Biographies

Émile Durkheim: Born in Epinal, in the Vosges region, on 15 April 1858. He studied at the lyceum Louis le Grand and later, in 1879, at the École Normale Supérieure, where he took the *agrégation* and received his degree in philosophy in 1882. For three years he was a *professeur agrégé* in the high schools; then he settled down in Paris beginning his collaboration with the *Revue philosophique*. In 1887 he moved to Bordeaux to teach at the Faculty of Letters a course in social science and education. In 1888 he published a remarkable study on suicide, mainly based on statistical reports. In 1893 he presented, as a doctoral dissertation, *De la division du travail social: étude sur l'organisation des sociétés supérieures*; in 1895 *Les règles de la méthode sociologique* appeared and the *Année sociologique* was started. In 1897 he published *Le suicide* in which the type and degree of social solidarity are viewed as determinants of what appears to be a purely individual behavior. In 1912 he published his last major work, *Les formes élémentaires de la vie religieuse: le système totémique en Australie*. Heartbroken over the death of his son André on the Bulgarian front, he died on 15 November 1917.

Friedrich Engels: Born on 28 November 1820 in Barmen, Northern Germany, of a rich family, with interests in the textile industry. As a reaction against the conservative attitude of his family, in 1840 he joined the left-wing Young Hegelians. He met for the first time Marx in Köln in 1842; in the next year, he started to work at the Ermen and Engels textile factory in Manchester where he became acquainted with the English political economy in both theory and practice. In 1844 he published *The Condition* *of the Working Class in England*. In Paris, in 1844, he met Marx a second time, and this was the beginning of a great friendship and constant cooperation. In 1845 he worked with Marx to write *The German Ideology*, to be published only posthumously. In 1852 he shared with Marx the political isolation following the dissolution of the Communist League. In 1877 he published *Anti-dühring* and in 1884 *The Origin of the Family, Private Property and the State*. In 1885 and 1894 he published the second and the third volumes of *Capital*. He died in 1895.

Adam Ferguson: Born in Logierat, Scotland, in 1723. He received his first education at the parish school where his father was serving as pastor; later, he enrolled at the Grammar School of Perth and in 1739 he registered at the University of Saint Andrews, specializing in classical literature as well as in philosophy and mathematics. In 1743 he received his degree and, in order to please his father, chose an ecclesiastical career. In 1745 he became chaplain of the Black Watch regiment; nine years later, at the death of his father, he abandoned the ecclesiastical state to devote himself completely to teaching and research. In 1756 he published anonymously *Reflections Previous to the Establishment of a Militia* in which he proposes the organization of a Scottish army. In 1759 he was awarded the chair of natural philosophy at the University of Edinburgh. Finally, in 1764, he was able to occupy the chair of moral philosophy. In 1766 he married Katherine Burnett. His most famous book was published in 1767 under the title *An Essay on the History of Civil Society*, followed, two years later, by *Institutes of Moral Philosophy*, and, in 1783, by *The History of the Progress and Termination of the Roman Republic* and by *Principles of Moral and Political Science* in 1792. In order to prepare the second edition of his work on the Roman Republic he visited, in 1793, Germany and Italy, residing for some time in Rome. He died on 22 February 1816 at Saint Andrews.

Karl Marx: Born on 5 May 1818 in Trier, Prussia. In 1835 he enrolled at the University of Bonn to study law; then, at the University of Berlin in the milieu of the *Doktorklub*, in which he became familiar with Hegelian philosophy. His doctoral dissertation, discussed in 1841, concerned the difference between the philosophy of Democritus and Epicurus. In 1842 he began his collaboration with the *Rheinische Zeitung* and in 1843, having married Jenny von Westphalen, he settled down in Paris; together with Arnold Ruge, he edited the *Deutsch-Französische Jahrbücher*, of which only one issue appeared and in which he published two essays: "On the Jewish Question" and the "Introduction to the Critique of Hegel's Philosophy of Right." In 1845 he transferred to Brussels and started a collaboration with Friedrich Engels, which became a lifelong friendship. In 1848, together with Engels, he published in Brussels the *Manifesto of the Commu-*

nist Party. After a brief stay in Paris, Marx and his family moved to London, destined to remain their hometown. In 1852 he published *The Eighteenth Brumaire of Louis Bonaparte*. Through 1857 he lived in great poverty, helped to an extent by Engels. In 1867 he published the first volume of *Capital*. The International Working Men's Association, internally divided, was transferred to New York and finally dissolved in 1876. He died on 14 March 1883.

Vilfredo Pareto: Born in Paris on 15 July 1848 of an aristocratic family originally from Genoa. Ten years later the family moved back to Italy and Pareto studied at the University of Turin, where he received a degree in mathematics and physics in 1867. In 1869 he defended successfully a dissertation on the "Fundamental Principles of the Theory of Elasticity in Solid Bodies and Fundamental Researches on the Integration of the Differential Equations which Define their Equilibrium." His first work experience was in Rome as an engineer for iron and steel mills. In 1874 Pareto settled in Florence in a managerial position; he was favorable to a laissez-faire political economy, and it is no wonder that he was a prominent member of the Adam Smith Society. In 1891, having met the Italian economist Maffeo Pantaleoni, Pareto turned his scientific interests to economics and, in 1893, through the recommendation of Pantaleoni, he succeeded Léon Walras at the chair of political economy at the University of Lausanne. In 1901 he published *Les systèmes socialistes* and finally, from 1916 to 1919, the *Trattato di sociologia generale* (*Compendium of General Sociology*) appeared. He died in Lausanne on 19 August 1923.

Pierre-Joseph Proudhon: Born in Besançon on 15 January 1809, of a poor provincial family, in constant struggle against the arrogance of the wealthy. In 1820 he obtained a scholarship that allowed him to attend the Besançon college as a student externe. In 1827 he was forced to abandon his studies in order to help the family. He became a typical self-taught scholar. He was hired, in 1833, as a typographical worker in a Besançon firm. In 1830 he went to Paris with another scholarship. His first essay on property, which he dedicated to the Besançon Academy, was rejected. A second essay, again on property, was dedicated to Louis Blanqui. In 1842 Proudhon published a third version of the essay on property, with the famous statement *la propriété c'est un vol* ("property is a theft") and was denounced for inciting the people against poverty and government. In 1845, after an exchange of letters, there was a bitter breakup with Marx, who later would attack Proudhon's doctrine, especially as stated in his *La philosophie de la misère*, with a polemical tract "La misère de la philosophie". In 1858 he published *De la justice dans la révolution et dans l'eglise* that earned him three years in prison. In 1864 he wrote *Lettre aux ouvriers* and began *De la capacité politique de la classe ouvrière*. He died at Passy, where he had settled upon his return from Belgium, on 19 January 1865.

Claude-Henri de Saint-Simon: Born in Paris on 17 October 1760; a nephew of Louis de Rouvroy, duc de Saint-Simon, famous author of the *Mémoirs*. He led an adventurous life, partly spent in the army (he was seriously wounded in the battle of Les Saintes and taken prisoner in 1783) and partly in risky commercial enterprises that often failed quite miserably. In 1787, in Spain, he tried to convince the Spanish government to build a channel that would make Madrid a seaport. The French Revolution began while he was still in Spain (1789); when he returned to France in 1790, Saint-Simon renounced his title and aristocratic privileges. He assumed the name of Claude-Henri Bonhomme, but this did not prevent the authorities of the Revolution from putting him in jail "for general security reasons." He regained his freedom in 1794. After some unfortunate commercial ventures, in 1802 he began his literary production with an anonymous letter *A la société du Lycée* in which he advocates a general theory of all the sciences. *Lettre aux Européens* and *Lettre d'un habitant de Genève á l'humanité* followed in the same year. A book *Essai sur l'organisation sociale* made him suspect in the eyes of the police. During 1806 and 1807, to support himself, he accepted an administrative post at the Mont de Piété while studying at night. In 1810 he published in Paris *Esquisse d'une nouvelle Encyclopédie ou Introduction à la philosophie du XIXme siècle*. In a limited edition he published in 1813 *Mémoire sur la science de l'homme* and *Travail sur la gravitation universelle*. In 1814 one of his most important works appeared under the title *De la réorganisation de la société européenne*. In 1817 and 1818 four volumes of *Industrie* appeared and in 1820 the complete edition of *L'organizateur* was published, followed, in 1822, by *Du système industriel*. He died on 19 May 1825, after having finished *Nouveau Christianisme*.

Georg Simmel: Born in Berlin on 1 March 1858. He graduated Berlin's Humboldt University in philosophy, history of art, and history. His doctoral dissertation concerned *Das Wesen der Materie nach Kants physischer Monadologie* (The Essence of Matter according to Kant's Physical Monadology). In 1882 he published in *Zeitschrift für Völkerpsychologie und Sprachwissenschaft*, an essay, *Psychologisch-ethnographische Studien über die Anfänge der Musik* (Psychological-Ethnographic Studies on the Origins of Music). His first book was published in 1890 under the title *Über soziale Differenzierung* (On Social Differentiation), followed in 1892 by *Die Probleme der Geschichtsphilosophie* (The Problems of the Philosophy of History) and, in 1900, by *Philosophie des Geldes* (*The Philosophy of Money*). Anti-Semitism as well as his brilliance were powerful obstacles to his career advancement. But his scientific production was impressive: *Kant*, in 1904; *Soziologie*, in 1908; *Haupt Probleme der Philosophie* (Fundamental Problems of Philosophy) in 1910; *Das Problem der historischen Zeit* (The Problem of Historical Time); *Rembrandt*, in 1916, and *Grundfragen der Soziologie* (Fundamental Issues of Sociology), in 1917. Appointed finally at the University of Strasburg, he died, before becoming full professor, on 28 September 1918.

Werner Sombart: Born in Ermsleber Harz, Germany, on 19 January 1863. He was among the founders of the Deutsche Gesellschaft für Soziologie (German Association of Sociology) in 1909 and in the same year he published a biography of Karl Marx, *Das Lebenswerk von Karl Marx*. As Professor at the Higher Business School in Berlin in 1917, it was not until 1927 that he published the third and last volume of his major work *Der Moderne Kapitalismus* (*Modern Capitalism*). He was elected president of the Verein für Sozialpolitik (Association for the Study of Social Politics) which he dissolved in order to save it from Nazi control. He died in Berlin on 19 May 1941.

Gabriel Tarde: Born in Sarlat (Dordogne, France) on 10 March 1843. In 1860 he was awarded his degree at a college of Jesuits; because of a serious disease, he could not enroll in the École Polytechnique, but he attended in Toulouse the Faculty of Law. In 1873 he was appointed magistrate, but after two years he returned to Sarlat and published his major work *Les lois de l'imitation*, followed, in 1879, by a literary book, *Comtes et poèmes*. In 1894 he was appointed chief officer of criminal statistics at the Ministry of Justice and published his second major work, *La logique sociale*. In 1900, encouraged by his friends Théodore Ribot and Louis Liard, he accepted a university position in Paris. He died suddenly on 12 May 1904.

Richard Henry Tawney: Born in Calcutta on 30 November 1880. His father held the chair of Sanscrit at the Presidency College. In 1903 Tawney finished his studies at Balliol College and obtained "a Second in Greats." After his degree, he worked in the slums of the "East End" of London and became an active member of the Workers' Educational Association. In 1912 he published a major work under the title *The Agrarian Problem in the Sixteenth Century*. In 1915 he was drafted into the army as a private and was seriously injured in 1916. After the war, he went on with his social and educational work and in 1920 published *The Acquisitive Society*; later, in 1925, he published *The British Labour Movement* and *Discourse upon Usury*. Despite his political involvement in the general strike of 1926, he was able to publish in the same year *Religion and the Rise of Capitalism*, in which he reformulates Weber's thesis in *The Protestant Ethic and the Spirit of Capitalism*. In 1931 he became professor of economic history at the London School of Economics and Political Science. As a result of his journey to China in 1932, he published *Land and Labour in China*, and in 1953 a memoir of the First World War, *The Attack, and other Papers*. He died in London on 16 January 1962.

Thorstein Veblen: Born in 1857 near Cato, Wisconsin (in Manitowoc County), on a farm, of a Norwegian immigrant family. In 1874 he enrolled at Carleton College, in Northfield, where his brother Andrew was also a student. In 1880 he obtained his Bachelor of Arts and in 1884 he earned his doctorate with a dissertation on "The Ethical Foundations of a Doctrine of Reward." In the same year he published an essay in the *Journal of Speculative Philosophy* on Kant's critique of judgment. After several academic wanderings, he published in Chicago *The Theory of the Leisure Class*, in 1899, a book that made him famous and at the same time misled many of his readers who were unable to understand the serious arguments often couched by Veblen in sardonic formulas. His scientific production, however, continued with *The Theory of Business Enterprise* (1904), *The Instinct of Workmanship* (1914), *Imperial Germany and the Industrial Revolution* (1915), *The Nature of Peace* (1916). In 1919 he wrote extensively and always provocatively for the New York journal *The Dial*. He died in Menlo Park, California, on 3 August 1929.

Max Weber: Born in Erfurt on 21 April 1864 of an upper-class family with keen interests in politics. In 1869 he moved with his family to Berlin; his home was frequently visited by some of the major social scientists, mostly historians and economists of the time. In 1882 he enrolled at the University of Heidelberg in the School of Law and in 1889 presented his doctoral dissertation *Zur Geschichte der Handelsgesellschaften im Mittelalter* (On the History of Medieval Business Organizations). He developed a strong interest in social issues which brought him to the Verein für Sozialpolitik. Weber qualified for his *Privatdozent* in 1892 with the essay *Die römische Agrargeschichte in iihrer Bedeutung für das Staats- und Privatrecht* (Roman Agrarian History and Its Meaning for Public- and Private Law). In 1894 he was awarded the chair in political economy at the University of Freiburg; later, in 1896, he was appointed at the University of Heidelberg to succeed Karl Knies as professor of political economy. In 1898 he was forced to leave his teaching commitments on account of poor health. In 1903 he renounced university teaching and accepted the editorship, together with Werner Sombart, of the *Archiv für Sozialwissenschaft und Sozialpolitik*. His basic works were published in 1904: *Die Objektivät sozialwissenschaftlicher und sozialpolitischer Erkenntnis* and *Die protestantische Ethik und der "Geist" das Kapitalismus*. In 1908 he wrote the methodological introduction to the research on the "selection and adaptation of workpower to large-scale industry." In 1909 he was among the founders of the Deutsche Gesellschaft für Soziologie. In 1913 *Über einige Kategorien der verstehenden Soziologie* was published while fundamental studies on the sociology of world religions were prepared. In 1918 he actively participated in the elaboration of the constitution of the Weimar Republic; professor, finally, in Munich, he delivered his famous *Wissenschaft als Beruf* and *Politik als Beruf* lectures. He died on 14 June 1920.

Index

+
About the Author

Franco Ferrarotti was born in Piedmont, Italy, in 1926. He graduated the University of Turin in 1949 with a dissertation on "The Sociology of Thorstein Veblen." In the same year, his translation of Veblen's *The Theory of the Leisure Class* was published by Einaudi and was savagely attacked by Benedetto Croce in *Corriere della Sera* of 15 January 1949. Ferrarotti replied with two essays in the *Rivisita di Filosofia* and earned national prominence. An independent member of the Italian Parliament from 1958 to 1963, he did not stand for reelection in order to devote himself to scientific research. In 1960 he was awarded the first full-time chair in sociology established in the Italian university system. In 1965 he was a Fellow at the Center for Advanced Study in the Behavioral Sciences at Palo Alto, California. In 1978 he was appointed Directeur d'Études at the Maison des Sciences de l'Homme and École des Hautes Études en Sciences Sociales in Paris. He is presently professor of sociology and a director of the doctoral program at the University of Rome, Faculty of Sociology. Several of his books have been translated into English, French, Spanish, and Japanese. In 1951 he founded, with Nicola Abbagnano, the *Quaderni di Sociologia*, which he edited until 1967; he is currently editor of *La Critica Sociologica*.